COME WHAT M

Scripture quotations are from the
King James Version of the Bible
All Greek and Hebrews definitions are
from the Strong's Exhaustive Concordance

You are welcome to copy portions of this book.
However, no portion is to be reproduced and sold.

May 18, 2020

Clarissa,
May you hear His voice on every page!
Love,
Peachy Ann

TABLE OF CONTENTS

Page

4	Dedication
5	After You have Suffered Awhile
14	An Odious Odor Has Lifted
17	As Jesus Passed By
29	Cousin Frank and the Country Cousin Doctor
33	The Crucifixion: A Medical View
44	End-Time Strategy
48	Father, Forgive Me
59	How Great Is That Darkness
61	I Have Allowed This
63	I Left Off Dealing With Her Fifty Years Ago
65	In Honor of Geneva Martin
68	It Was A Serious Non-Issue Issue
70	I've Killed Thousands
73	Knowledge, Falsely So Called
75	Look What God Gave
76	Lord, Save These Gamblers
78	Man Made To Worship
81	Margaret Knew It Was Real

84	Oh, Boy, That's My Kind of Scripture!
87	The Worst Assignment
92	The Next Worst Assignment
95	Our Little Secret
98	Pa Ford Plowed Straight
102	The Conversion of Paul
114	Plan With Prayer
117	Prayer Secrets Revealed
121	Testimonies From Long Ago
132	The Enoch Testimony
134	Theory Verses Experience
136	There Remaineth, Therefore, a Rest
140	The Reverend Ike
142	They All Told the Truth
155	Trust or Thrust
163	Watch and Pray
171	We Don't Drink Coffee In This Church!
173	We'll Take Him In a Heartbeat!
175	Why a Fox?
179	Words Paint a Picture
182	Wrapped In White Linen
185	You Can't Have It!

DEDICATION

In our ever-changing world, it's wonderful to know that our God is God, He is God alone, He is God enough, and He changes not.

Malachi 3:6 For I am thee Lord, I change not ...

Understanding God's word and applying it to our hearts gives us the glorious peace God desires for His people.

When acknowledging the brevity of life, Moses wrote in the only psalm attributed to him:
   Psalm 90:12 So teach us to number our days, that we might apply our hearts unto wisdom.

It is hoped that you will discover gems of God's wisdom throughout, "Come What May, He's Always God."

By: Gladys Goldsby Ford

Cover Design: Kharis Courtney

Editor: G.W. Gonzales

AFTER YOU HAVE SUFFERED AWHILE

As we study scripture, the Holy Spirit quickens our spirits to comprehend what is being revealed through mere words. God's Words are Spirit, and they are life to all who love Him.

Peter wrote the following after having "been through the process" of God:

1st Peter 5:10 But the God of all grace, who hath called us unto his eternal glory by Christ Jesus, <u>after ye have suffered awhile</u>, make you perfect, stablish, strengthen, settle you.

Peter had come to know the God who had chosen to allow this process in his life. The carnal mind might think, "Oh, no, Lord. Let's talk this over. Settle all of my heart's concerns N-O-W, not after I have suffered awhile!" Psychologists know that man lives his life in avoidance of pain and that avoiding pain or suffering is fundamental to mankind. We instinctively avoid pain and suffering. Somewhere along our individual journey (the sooner the better), we learn that life is not like a bag of trail mix where we pick our favorite pieces and pitch the rest.

In order to better understand some of the ways God has ordained for man to become perfect, we need to consider the sequence of "suffer, stablish, strengthen, and settle." And, as we embrace the wisdom of God in allowing this "ordained sequence," we, like Peter, will have an unshakable faith in God.

A woman called one morning and said she was going to bring a surprise that evening. I wanted to know what it was, but she wouldn't tell me. She just said, "No, I'm making you s-u-f-f-e-r." I was thrilled because I had <u>misunderstood</u>. I thought she had said, "I'm making you s-u-p-p-e-r." You might say that ignorance was bliss that day. Ignorance is not bliss when it comes to not understanding the ways of God or His dealings with us as individuals.

Hearing Him speak your name is thrilling; however, if you hear Him speak it twice, it may mean you are in trouble.
In **Luke 22:31-32** Jesus addressed Peter as, "Simon, Simon." In other instances, He issued strong rebukes by saying, "Martha, Martha" and "Saul, Saul."

Luke 22:31-32 And the Lord said, Simon, Simon, behold, Satan hath desired to have you, that he may sift you as wheat. But I have prayed for thee, that thy faith fail not. And when thou art converted, <u>strengthen thy brethren</u>.

It is curious that the only scripture where Jesus called him "Peter" is in verse 34 of the same discourse. He may have done this as a way of further "shoring him up" for the sifting that was to come. Peter is a Greek word (#4074) meaning, "petros, a piece of a rock." It's as though He was saying, "Peter, you are not to worry. I have prayed your faith will not fail during your time of sifting. You are a piece of the Rock." Other scriptures tell us plainly that the Rock is our Lord Jesus.

NOTE: The seventeen scriptures referring to Jesus as a Rock are too numerous to list here.

Peter was as the wheat, and his self-confidence was as the chaff. Notice that Jesus said He had <u>already prayed</u> for him. And we know now that Jesus ever-liveth to make intercession on our behalf as well. **(Hebrews 7:25)**

In this one short verse (Luke 22:31-32), we learn that Jesus had agreed to allow the process. He didn't pray for Peter to be delivered from the sifting of Satan. He prayed only that his faith would not fail and that through the sifting he would be converted or turned about and then be able to strengthen his brethren. Jesus knew the "getting through it" would be rough but that the end result would be glorious.

This conversion process wasn't just for Peter. Jesus when speaking to His disciples said:
Matthew 18:3-4 Verily, I say unto you, Except ye be <u>converted</u>, and become as little children, ye shall not enter into the kingdom of heaven. Whosoever, therefore, shall humble himself as this little child, the same is the greatest in the kingdom of heaven.

Through the sifting, Jesus desired Peter to be converted and become, not childish, but childlike. Peter's focus had to be turned from self-serving to God-serving. Here are some of the questions and statements of Peter before he was <u>converted</u> (or turned about).

Matthew 18:21 (Peter speaking) Lord, how often shall my brother sin against me, and I forgive him? Until seven times?

Peter did not have a clue of how greatly he would sin against the Lord. Neither do we know what our testing will reveal, but we know God will bring us through.

Matthew 19:27 Then answered Peter and said unto him, Behold, we have forsaken all, and followed thee. What shall we have, therefore?
Matthew 26:33 Peter answered and said unto him, Though all men shall be offended because of thee, yet will I never be offended.
Luke 9:28-33 And it came to pass, about eight days after these sayings, that he took Peter and John and James, and went up into a mountain to pray. And as he prayed, the appearance of his countenance was altered, and his raiment was white and glistening. And, behold, there talked to him two men, who were Moses and Elijah, who appeared in glory, and spoke of his decease <u>which he should accomplish</u> at Jerusalem. But Peter, and they that were with him, were heavy with sleep; and when they were awake, they saw his glory, and the two men that stood with him. And it came to pass, as they departed from him, that Peter said unto Jesus, 'Master, it is good for us to be here; let us make three booths: one for thee, and one for Moses, and one for Elijah, <u>not knowing what he said</u>.

The reason Peter's attitudes and behaviors are pointed out is so we can better appreciate the changes that were to be brought about by the hewing process of God. Those who fear God and desire to be pleasing unto Him, do quite a bit of changing throughout their lifetime.

Psalm 55:19 ..... because they have no changes (or do not change,) therefore, they fear not God.

God wants His people to be continually changed and renewed as they become more Christ-like. Peter's walk and talk recorded in the gospels are in direct contrast to his writings in 1st and 2nd Peter. He did a lot of changing over the course of his life, just as all sincere followers of Christ do.

In **1st Peter 1:4**, he spoke of the exceedingly great and precious promises God gave that we might be partakers of the divine nature. Sadly, we live in a time when many with covetous desires cloak them by "claiming the promises of God" as a way of obtaining worldly prosperity without submitting to the process of being perfected by Him.

Before situations were allowed to humble him, Peter was not willing to suffer, but he was to learn that suffering can bring joy. And, what is J-O-Y other than putting **J**esus first, **O**thers second, and **Y**ourself last.

Acts 5:41 And they (Peter and the other apostles) departed from the presence of the council, rejoicing that they were counted worthy to suffer shame for his name.

Peter spoke the following words at Jerusalem as he challenged fellow-Jews to receive Jesus:

Acts 3:19 Repent, therefore, and be <u>converted</u>, that your sins may be blotted out, when (literally "so that") the times of refreshing shall come from the presence of the Lord.

Notice that Peter chose to use the word <u>converted</u>, which is the same word Jesus had spoken to him. He had been "through the process" and was now busy strengthening his brethren.

When we understand more of the processes God allows for our perfection (not for our destruction), we are better able to cooperate with Him and to cherish His promise to perfect that which concerns us.

All through the process of "suffer, stablish, strengthen, settle," He's working His very best on your behalf. And, His very best results in, not only you being converted or turned about, but also in you being able to strengthen your brethren. (☺Yeah!)

Proverbs 22:19-21 That thy trust may be in the Lord, I have made known to thee this day, even to thee. Have I not written to thee excellent things in counsels and knowledge, that I may make thee know the certainty of the words of truth, that thou mightest answer the words of truth, to those who send unto thee?

Through the process of suffering, our trust is turned from ourselves and others to the Creator God.

Speaking of suffering, **Hebrews 5:8-9** reminds us:
Though he were a son, yet he learned obedience by the things which he suffered; and being made perfect, he became the author of eternal salvation unto all them that obey him.

Notice the connection between "suffering" and "being made perfect." What we consider "suffering" is allowed for our perfection; not for our destruction.

In the following verses, Paul used the words <u>suffer</u> and <u>glory</u> each twice.
    Romans 8:17-18 ... if so be that we <u>suffer</u> with him, that we may also be <u>glorified</u> together. For I reckon that the <u>sufferings</u> of this present time are not worthy to be compared with the <u>glory</u> which shall be revealed in us.

Paul also acknowledged this connection:
    2nd Timothy 2:12 (Written by Paul) If we suffer, we shall also reign with him ...

The work of becoming "strengthened and settled" is evident in the ministry of Peter recorded in Acts where his name is mentioned fifty-six times in the first fifteen chapters. Now that he had been converted, the Holy Spirit was able to perform the works of God through him. He will do the same in your life, my friend, as you allow the process of perfection.

It's believed that 1st Peter was written 60 A.D. and 2nd Peter approximately six years later. The depth of Peter's understanding had increased tremendously during those years, just as ours does when we continue in steadfast perseverance. 1st Peter has been called "the epistle of joyful hope." It provides believers with a divine and eternal perspective of their earthly life and serves to remind them that they have a glorious calling and an inheritance in Jesus. Peter cautioned saints that their faith and love of God would be subjected to testing and refining but that all of this would result in praise, glory, and honor at the appearing of the Lord. **(1st Peter 1:7)** Peter knew what he was talking about. He had truly lived his message, just as we do.

Father God, the Master Communicator, delights in His people discovering His ways of communicating through His word and by His Spirit. One of the ways God chooses to honor His people is by mentioning them by name. He may be dishonoring someone by not mentioning their name. Only one scripture recognized Bath-sheba as King David's wife. Other scriptures refer to her as the "wife of Uriah," or as "Uriah's wife." Could this be a hint?

Matthew 1:6 And Jesse beget David the king; and David the king beget Solomon of her who had been the wife of Uriah.

You might think, "Well, that's the begets, and the begets are masculine." Not so; there are four women named in the begets, and one of them was a harlot. The point is that God chose to honor the harlot Rahab by mentioning her name. He chose to honor Uriah by mentioning his name, and He chose NOT to honor Bath-sheba. Spotting these things enables us to understand more of God's way of communicating through His word. It's also important to notice the order He chooses when listing names. Matthew 10:2, Mark 3:16, Luke 6:13, Acts 1:13 all list the twelve apostles (with the exception of Acts 1:13, because there were only eleven at that time). Which apostle do you suppose is always mentioned first? Which disciple do you suppose is always listed last? ☺

Matthew 10:2 Now the names of the twelve apostles are these, <u>the first Simon, who is called Peter</u>…"

Is it a coincidence that all scriptures listing the twelve apostles list Peter <u>first</u> and Judas Iscariot <u>last</u>? Yes, God chose to honor Peter by always mentioning his name first. And yes, Peter had to undergo a lot of "perfecting" before writing 1st and 2nd Peter years later.

It's interesting that in **1st Peter 5:2** he encouraged others to "feed the flock of God" just as Jesus had instructed him to "feed my sheep."

Peter had come to understand and appreciate the divine sequence of "suffer, stablish, strengthen, and settle" as one of the ways God uses to perfect His children. As we walk with the Lord and identify the necessary sequence of events He has chosen to allow for our perfection, we rejoice in His sovereign care.

AN ODIOUS ODOR HAS LIFTED

Martin glanced at the church and grounds as he drove by. When the Lord spoke, he did a double-take of the scene and wondered what had transpired. The Lord had let him know, "An odious odor has lifted."

He knew "odious" a Hebrew word (#8130) meant "utterly hateful" from studying Proverbs 30 where it's written:
Proverbs 30:21-23 For three things the earth is disquieted, and for four things which it cannot bear: For a servant when he reigneth; and a fool when he is filled with food; for <u>an odious woman when she is married</u> ...

Part of the deception of an "odious woman" is that the poor fella doesn't know his bride is odious until she says, "I do," and then doesn't.

Martin had recently left the church where the odious pastor's wife, Bonita, ruled and reigned. He soon learned on the grape-vine that the pastor had resigned and he and his family had moved out of the area. This was that pastor's third and final church resignation.

Sitting in a front row pew, worshipers had felt Bonita's heart-piercing arrows directed at her husband. At times, he would become confused and lose his thoughts while speaking to the small congregation. The conflict in their marriage was troubling. She loathed him pastoring and held him hostage by reminding him of his days as a serial cheater. Bonita was his true nemesis dedicated to the goal of him forsaking his calling, which many believe he truly had. Rather than working in the Kingdom of God winning souls, she urged him to seek employment to make their family more financially secure.

Martin and others had been aware of this marital charade of two unequally yoked spouses trapped in a miserable power struggle that made their marriage a hamster wheel journey. Martin and others joined in fatiguing battle-royale prayer for this couple and for the church. Their intersession only muddied the waters engaging and enraging the demonic forces working to defeat this P.O.W. pastor-husband.

A woman from their prayer group had a dream; a disturbing dream. In the dream, she had come to the church and found emaciated unclean babies crawling on the floor throughout the church crying for help. Bonita was there, so she summonsed her help. "We have to get all these babies to a hospital quick. Help me," the woman pleaded. With a wave of her hand, Bonita carelessly said, "Oh, let them alone. They'll be okay." It's believed that this dream depicted the true reality.

The Lord again spoke to Martin some months later: You were sent there to cut off the House of Ahab. That's an assignment he would have preferred be given to someone else. But God had had enough and used him to take an uncompromised stance, which helped usher this ministry couple's exit.

Martin saw this former-ministry couple at a funeral wake a decade later. He afterward commented that the now satisfied Bonita looked like "the cat that ate the canary." Her husband's appearance was that of the carcass of a hot air balloon. He had done well in his real estate business and other pursuits. This now successful couple lived in an upscale elite area of their new town.

Mark 8:36 For what shall it profit a man, if he shall gain the whole world, and lose his own soul?

1st Timothy 6: ... supposing that gain is godliness; from such withdraw thyself. But godliness with contentment is much gain.

Matthew 6:24 No man can serve two masters; for either he will hate the one, and love the other; or else he will hold to the one, and despise the other. Ye cannot serve God and money.

Remember, dear saint, those who love and serve God will have eternal retirement benefits that are out of the world!

AS JESUS PASSED BY

Gospel of John

Study of Chapter Nine

Before beginning our study of chapter 9, let's consider the combative discourse between Jesus and Pharisees recorded in chapter 8.

The Jews had accused Him of having a demon because He declared that God was His Father. They continued to assert that they were righteous because Abraham was their father. **(John 8:52)**

Speaking of His Father, Jesus said in **John 8:55**, "Yet ye have not known him; but I know him. And if I should say I know him not, I shall be a liar like unto you; but I know him, and keep his saying." He plainly told them that, although they were Pharisees and well-educated in the Law of Moses, they knew not God and that they were liars for claiming that they did know Him.

8:56-59 Your father, Abraham, rejoiced to see my day; and he saw it, and was glad. Then said the Jews unto him, Thou art not yet fifty years old, and hast thou seen Abraham? Jesus said unto them, Verily, verily, I say unto you, Before Abraham <u>was</u>, **I am**.

The ever-existent Jesus is evermore present and is never referred to in the past-tense.

8:59 Then took they up stones to cast at him; but Jesus hid himself, and went out of the temple, going through the midst of them, and so passed by.

Let's appreciate how casually this event is recorded. After the intense confrontation with religious leaders, Jesus merely departed by going through the midst of them and so passed by. Going on to Chapter 9 where a seemingly causal happenstance transpired, we find another instance where Jesus "passed by."

9:1 And as Jesus passed by, he saw a man who was blind from his birth.

This man was born-blind whereas the religious leaders were made blind by their vain traditions and their lack of true knowledge of God. We are soon to learn that what appeared to be a coincidental encounter was actually a divine appointment. (You will have a few of these in your life, too).

9:2 And his disciples asked him, saying, Master, who did sin, this man or his parents, that he was born blind?

His disciples, still locked in a biased religious mindset, only thought of two possibilities; the first of which is an absolute no-brainer. They asked a no-brainer question:

had this born-blind man sinned to cause his blindness. Think about it. Did they believe he sinned sometime before he was born? Duh. The view that his parents' sin may have caused him to be born-blind is not a notion we will consider here. Even today, some feel that calamity or misfortune is a result of God's disfavor. We do not choose the circumstance of our birth and neither did this man. Surely he would not have chosen to be born-blind, to live throughout childhood and into manhood not seeing, and to only exist as a blind beggar. And, yet, we will see that the all-knowing God had chosen this for him <u>until the time when Jesus passed by</u>. That's a heavy thought.

9:3 Jesus answered, Neither hath this man sinned, nor his parents, but that the works of God should be made manifest in him.

Without rebuke, He silenced their speculation by clearly stating the man's condition was not caused by anyone's sin. It was the result of God's desire to manifest His glory through the man's pitiful state. This unnamed man learned in a moment of time that his condition was ordained by God. He had only experienced underserved hardship. He had not been blessed with wealth but he was to become richer than the richest man; for God had ordained that His glory be revealed through the healing of his miserable condition. This should encourage us not to fret over dilemmas or trials that we feel are undeserved. Believers should allow God to manifest His glory through what might be seen as adversity.

9:4-6 I must work the works of him that sent me, while it is yet day; the night cometh, when no man can work. As long as I am in the world, I am the light of the world. When he had thus spoken, he spat on the ground, and made clay of the spittle, and anointed the eyes of the blind man with the clay.

This may remind you of the times your mother spit on you to sort of clean you up a bit. Jesus used His own spit in healing a deaf man. **(Mark 7:33)** He also used His spit to heal a blind man. **(Mark 8:23)** He could have used any means but choose His own DNA.

9:7 And he said unto him, Go, wash in the pool of Siloam (which is by interpretation, Sent). He went his way, therefore, and washed, and came seeing.

The born-blind man quickly obeyed and received his sight without ever asking to be healed. He didn't, at this time, know who Jesus was; but he was soon to learn.

9:8-9 The neighbors, therefore, and they who before had seen him that he was blind, said, Is not this he who sat and begged? Some said, This is he; others said, he is like him; <u>but he said, I am he</u>.

I like this man. He replied in a straight forward manner when questioned by neighbors. He'll be even straighter forward when robustly interrogated by the Pharisees.

You'll appreciate the heart of this unnamed formerly-blind man as scripture reveals not only his heart but the heart of all involved. Revealing hearts; isn't that what the God-ordained happenings in our lives do?

9:10-17 Therefore said they unto him, How were thine eyes opened? He answered, and said, A man who is called Jesus made clay, and anointed mine eyes, and said unto me, Go to the pool of Siloam, and wash; and I went and washed, and I received sight. Then said they unto him, Where is he? And he said, I know not. They brought to the Pharisees him that formerly was blind. And it was the Sabbath day when Jesus made the clay, and opened his eyes. Then again the Pharisees asked him how he had received his sight. He said unto them, He put clay upon mine eyes, and I washed, and do see. Therefore said some of the Pharisees, This man is not of God, because he keepeth not the Sabbath day. Others said, How can a man that is a sinner do such miracles? And there was a division among them. They say unto the blind man again, What sayest thou of him, since he hath opened thine eyes? He said, He is a prophet.

This precious now-seeing man repeated verbatim what he had told his neighbors. All we can do is repeat over and over what Jesus has done for us. No, we don't understand it all, but we, as Christians, can each give enthusiastic reports of what Jesus has done in our lives. We are not witnesses of a religious sect or organization. We are witnesses of what we have experienced. Yeah! ☺

Saying, "He is a prophet," evidenced his personal progressive (ongoing) revelation of Jesus, which will culminate with him worshiping Him as the Son of God. I pray that you are experiencing the pleasure of your own personal progressive revelation of Jesus the Messiah.

9:18-19 But the Jews did not believe concerning him, that he had been blind and received his sight, until they called the parents of him that had received his sight, And they asked them, saying, Is this your son, who ye say was born blind? How, then, doth he now see?

Those who study this event and who are effected by the Pharisees condescending callous arrogance will be even more effected by the born-blind man's parents. ☹

9:20-23 His parents answered them, and said, We know that this is our son, and that he was born blind; But by what means he now seeth, we know not; or who hath opened his eyes, we know not. He is of age; ask him. He will speak for himself. These words spoke his parents, because they feared the Jews; for the Jews had agreed already that, if any man did confess that he was Christ, he should be put out of the synagogue. Therefore said his parents, He is of age; ask him.

Our hearts ache for this born-blind beggar, when seeing his parents for the first time, must also have seen their fear of man overriding any gratitude that Jesus had "passed by." These parents had already been exonerated by Jesus saying their son's blindness had not been caused by their sin. Yet, the fear of man robbed them of the jubilation they could have had knowing their son would no longer be a blind beggar, he could now see clearly (including seeing them).

His parents weren't alone in fearing the rejection of man. Consider what John later recorded in:

John 12:42-43 Nevertheless, among the chief rulers also many believed on him; but because of the Pharisees they did not confess him, lest they should be put out of the synagogue ...

This "fear of rejection" can be a tremendous snare. We must remember what the Lord told us through **Isaiah 53:3**; that the Messiah would be despised and rejected of men. Those who are following in His footsteps should expect the same. Don't allow the fear of man to rob you of triumph in the Lord which is joy unspeakable. The remarkable boldness of the formerly-blind man has merited the admiration of countless millions (and with more added daily).

9:24-27 Then again called they the man that was blind, and said unto him, Give God the praise; we know that this man is a sinner. He answered, and said, Whether he is a sinner or not, I know not; one thing I know, whereas I was blind, now I see. Then said they unto him again, What did he do unto thee? How opened he thine eyes?

The Pharisees maintained steadfast denial that Jesus was the Son of God, and yet they could not deny the miracle. One purpose of their interrogation was to bully him into a compromised response like his parents had given. Well, it didn't work!

9:27 He answered them, I have told you already, and ye did not hear; why would you hear it again? Will ye also be his disciples?

Both of his questions boomeranged without the Pharisees giving a rebuttal. Imagine a formerly-blind beggar asking Pharisees such questions. Gotta love this man! He wasn't concerned of the opinions of others. He simply told what he knew to be true without fear of consequences. The conflict was in their minds, not his. After all, his parents said that he was of age and could speak for himself!

9:28-29 Then they reviled him, and said, Thou art his disciple; but we are Moses' disciples. We know that God spoke unto Moses; as for this fellow, we know not from hence he is.

Four scriptures tell of Jesus being "reviled" meaning He was abusively reproached. Reviled is a Greek word (#3058, 3060). **(Matthew 27:39, Mark 15:32, John 9:28, 1st Peter 2:23)** So this suddenly-seeing man is in good company being reviled by the spiritually-blind Pharisees.

9:30-33 The man answered, and said unto them, Why here is a marvelous thing, that ye know not from where he is, and yet he hath opened mine eyes. Now we know that God heareth not sinners; but if any man be a worshiper of God, and doeth his will, him he heareth. Since the age began was it not heard that any man opened the eyes of one born blind. If this man were not of God, he could do nothing.

Our suddenly-seeing hero marveled at their failure to see that a marvelous miracle had transpired. This word "marvellous," as spelled in the KJV Bible is Greek (#2298) and means "wonderful." It appears in scripture twenty-four times; twenty-three of those times it is used to describe God and His work. It is marvelous that this born-blind man had true knowledge of God. His experience could not be overruled by their religious argument, and neither can yours. When first questioned he said he was healed by a man called Jesus. Later, he said Jesus was a prophet. Now he declared that Jesus is of God. **(9:11, 17, 33)** He's come a long way, just as we have. But wait, in a few more verses, he'll be worshiping Jesus as Lord!

9:34-35 They answered, and said unto him, Thou wast altogether born in sins, and thou dost teach us? And they cast him out. Jesus heard that they had cast him out; and when he had found him, he said unto him, Dost thou believe on the Son of God?

The haughty unteachable Pharisees dismissed the evidence of Jesus' deity; that left the healed man's compromising parents in the synagogue and their son cast out. This doesn't resemble an amicable family. Hmm. This man was accustomed to being "cast out" by a society that didn't embrace blind beggars, but now he was cast out of his only link to God: the synagogue. None of this mattered to this precious man. Jesus, as the Good Shepherd, sought our cast out hero and found him. If you have been cast out by a person, family, or group because you received the Lord, rest assured that He is searching for you to heal and restore your heart.

4:36-38 He answered, and said, Who is he, Lord, that I might believe on him? And Jesus said unto him, Thou hast both seen him, and it is he that talketh with thee. And he said, Lord, I believe. And he worshiped him.

Our hero had acknowledged in verse 33 that the man who healed him was of God. But Jesus now asked him if he believed on the Son of God (God manifested in the flesh). He agreed that he did believe and he worshiped Him. There he is; a Jewish man worshiping a man as God just as the disciples did. **(Matthew 14:33)**

Yes, the now-seeing man may have had his link with the synagogue severed, but now he has a link worth having: an ever-lasting bond with the One who created all things seen and unseen.

Before this lesson is concluded let's consider that our hero's blindness was caused by God's desire to manifest Himself. He is God. Couldn't He have thought of some other way? What a raw deal this man got. How unfair! We might think these questions within ourselves but we surely wouldn't write them in a book. ☺

I saved a garment tag from a dress bought years ago because what was written on it made me think of the of our sovereignty Creator God.

The tag reads, *"This is a specially washed garment. Shading, streaking, and weaving irregularities are intentional. They should be in no way considered defects, rather they add to the character of the garment.*

God had woven an irregular feature into this unnamed born-blind beggar in order to accomplish the purpose of glorifying Himself and developing a resolute character within the man.

Could it be that what we see as misfortune is part of God's design to manifest Himself in and through us?

Later verses reveal that this woven-in character trait equipped him to overcome religion and to follow Jesus.

Oh, for the wisdom of God! His gratitude will be demonstrated by his determination to glorify God while being condemned by others, forsaken by his parents, and by being cast out of the synagogue.

Remember the words written in:

James 4:14 For what is your life? It is even a vapor that appeareth for a little time, and then vanishes away.

It may not seem like a vapor during your lifetime, but it will when you reach that golden shore.

COUSIN FRANK
and the
COUNTRY COUSIN DOCTOR

When anyone in our family doesn't feel well, they know right where to go. Cousin Reggie's many years as a country town's family physician had earned him the reputation of knowing what to do. Grumpy patients left his office smiling knowing he had heard their complaint and had known how to fix it.

I have left his office more than a few times after receiving one of his "don't ask shots." I never knew what was in the variety-pack injection; I just trusted that its content would take care of the problem and it always did. ☺

As I was leaving Reggie's office one day, I was surprised to see our mutual-cousin, Frank, entering with his wife. I hugged them both, and without my asking, Frank volunteered a list of his ailments and complaints. He looked depleted and discouraged. His ailments, though, didn't amount to doodle-squat; but his complaint aroused my curiosity. He grumbled that Reggie had ordered test after test that had left him exhausted.

When I later spoke with Reggie, I commented that Frank had grumbled about all of the testing. His only explanation was, "Oh, I ordered lots of tests to teach him not to complain.

Maybe, like me, you've wondered why you have been severely tested by the Lord or why He directed you to take the scenic route through life.

After delivering His people from Egyptian bondage and into the land He had sworn to give their fathers, He gave them instructions through Moses:

Deuteronomy 8:2-3 And thou shalt remember all the way which the Lord thy God led thee these forty years in the wilderness, to humble thee, and to test thee, to know what was in thine heart, whether thou would keep his commandment or not.

Yes, we do remember all the way that He has brought us from the slavery of sin. My forty year wilderness journey has humbled me as He intended. How about you?

These scriptures acknowledge that our reaction to His testing (or trials) displays our hearts. In a sense, He already knows what's in our hearts and He knows whether or not we'll keep His commandments. The tests (trials) of life show to us and to others what's in our hearts. It's not always pretty.

The Lord continued warning of the danger of forgetting who they had been and of where He had brought them from once He had blessed them as no other people had been blessed:

Deuteronomy 8:14-18 Then thine heart be lifted up, and thou forget the Lord thy God, who brought thee forth out of the land of Egypt, from the house of bondage; who led thee through that great and terrible wilderness, wherein were fiery serpents, and scorpions, and drought, where there was no water; who brought thee forth water out of the rock of flint; who fed thee in the wilderness with manna, which thy fathers knew not, that he might humble thee, and that he might test thee, <u>to do thee good in thy latter end</u>; and thou say in thine heart, My power and the might of mine hand hath gotten me this wealth. But thou shalt remember the Lord thy God ...

There is a great deal of truth to ponder in these few scriptures; some of which would curdle a carnal mind. As if being a slave in a heathen land wasn't misfortune enough, God liberated them and brought them through a grueling forty year journey where they experienced extreme hardship. Yikes! No wonder some said they would have been better off to remain slaves. **(Exodus 16:3)** They could not have imagined what God was doing for their eternal benefit, and neither can you during your pilgrimage.

Wisdom gleaned from a proverb shines a light on some of the earthly benefits of our experiences:

Proverbs 22:19-21 That thy trust may be in the Lord, I have made known to thee this day, even to thee. Have not I written to thee excellent things in counsels and knowledge, that I might make thee know the certainty of the words of truth, that thou mightest answer the words of truth to those who send unto thee?

In may not be much consolation to you while you are being tested. However, it will give you satisfying joy when you are able to "know the certainty of the words of truth" and are confidently able to answer people who want to know how you made it through.

The African-American pastor, Charles Tindley wrote well-beloved gospel hymns. A favorite written in 1916, "We'll Understand It Better By and By" contains this refrain:

> By and by, when the morning comes,
>
> When the saints of God are gathered home.
>
> We'll tell the story how we've overcome,
>
> For we'll understand it better by and by.

And, dear pilgrim, we will all understand it better by and by when that glorious morning comes and we enter the eternal day.

THE CRUCIFIXION: A Medical View

BY: Dr. C. Truman Davis

Several years ago, I became interested in the physical aspects of the passion, or suffering, of Jesus when I read an account of the crucifixion in Jim Bishop's book, "The Day Christ Died." I suddenly realized that I had taken the crucifixion more or less for granted all these years ... that I had grown callous to its horror by a too-easy familiarity with the grim details. It finally occurred to me that, as a physician, I did not even know the immediate cause of Christ's death. The gospel writers do not help much on this point. Since crucifixion and scourging were so common during their lifetimes, they undoubtedly considered a detailed description unneeded. For that reason we have only the concise words of the gospels: "Pilate, having scourged Jesus, delivered Him to them to be crucified ... and they crucified Him."

Despite the gospel accounts' silence on the details of Christ's crucifixion, many have looked into this subject in the past. In my personal study of the event from a medical viewpoint, I am indebted especially to Dr. Pierre Barbet, a French surgeon who did exhaustive historical and experimental research and wrote extensively on the topic.

An attempt to examine the infinite mind and spiritual suffering of the Incarnate God in atonement for the sins of fallen man is beyond the scope of this article. However, the physical aspects of our Lord's passion we can examine in some detail. What did the body of Jesus of Nazareth actually endure during those hours of torture?

The Method of Crucifixion

This question led first to a study of the practice of crucifixion itself – that is, the torture and execution of a person by fixation to a cross. Apparently, the first known use of crucifixion was among the Persians. Alexander and his generals brought the practice of crucifixion to the Mediterranean world, to Egypt and to Carthage. The Romans evidently learned the technique from the Carthaginians and, as with most everything the Romans did, they rapidly developed a very high degree of efficiency and skill in carrying it out. A number of Roman authors have written on this subject.

Several methods are described in the ancient literature. Only a few have some relevance here. The upright portion of the cross, or stalk, could have the cross-arm, or patibulum, attached two or three feet below its top. This is what we commonly think of today as the classical form of the cross, usually named the Latin cross.

The common form used in Jesus' day, however, was the tau cross, shaped like the Greek letter tau τ or like our letter T. On this cross, the patibulum was placed in a notch at the top of the stalk. There is excellent archaeological evidence that it was on this type of cross that Jesus was crucified.

The upright post of the cross, however, was generally permanently fixed in the ground at the site of execution.

The condemned man was forced to carry the patibulum, apparently weighing about 110 pounds, from the prison to the place of execution. Without any historical or biblical proof, however, medieval and renaissance painters have given us our picture of Christ carrying the entire cross. Many painters and most of the sculptors of crucifixes also make a mistake in showing the nails driven through the palms. Roman historical accounts and experimental work have shown that the nails were driven between the small bones of the wrists and not through the palms. Nails driven through the palm will strip out between the fingers when they support the weight of a human body. This misconception may have come about through a misunderstanding of Jesus' words to Thomas, "Observe my hands." Modern and ancient anatomists, however, have always considered the wrist as a part of the hand.

A title or small sign stating the victim's crime was usually carried at the front of the procession and later was nailed to the cross above his head. This sign, with its staff nailed to the top of the cross would have given it somewhat the characteristic form of the Latin cross.

The physical passion of Christ began in Gethsemane, of the many aspects of this initial suffering, the one, which is of particular interest, is the bloody sweat. Interestingly enough, the physician Luke is the only gospel writer to mention this occurrence. He says, "And being in agony, he prayed more earnestly; and his sweat was, as it were, great drops of blood falling down to the ground."
Luke 22:44

Every attempt imaginable has been used by modern scholars to explain away the bloody sweat, apparently under the mistaken impression that it simply does not occur. A great deal of effort could be saved by consulting the medical literature. Though very rare, bloody sweat, is well documented. Under great emotional stress, tiny capillaries in the sweat glands can break, thus mixing blood with sweat. This process alone could have produced marked weakness and possible shock. Although Jesus' betrayal and arrest are important portions of the passion story, the next event in the account, which is significant from a medical perspective, is His trial before the Sanhedrin and Caiaphas, the High Priest. Here the first physical trauma was inflicted. A soldier struck Jesus across the face for remaining silent when questioned by Caiaphas. The palace guards then blindfolded Him, mockingly taunted Him to identify them as each passed by, spat on Him, and struck Him in the face.

Before Pilate
In the early morning, battered and bruised, dehydrated, and worn out from a sleepless night, Jesus was taken across Jerusalem to the commander of the Fortress Antonia, the seat of government of Judea, Pontius Pilate. We are familiar with Pilate's action in attempting to shift responsibility to Herod Antipas, the Tetrarch of Judea. Jesus apparently suffered no physical mistreatment at the hands of Herod, and was to returned Pilate. It was then, in response to the outcry of the mob, that Pilate

ordered Barabbas released and condemned Jesus to scourging and crucifixion.

There is much disagreement among authorities about scourging as a prelude to crucifixion. Most Roman writers from this period do not associate the two. Many scholars believe that Pilate originally ordered Jesus scourged as His full punishment and that the death sentence by crucifixion came only in response to the taunts by the mob that the governor was not properly defending Caesar against this pretender who claimed to be the King of the Jews.

It is doubtful whether the Romans made any attempt to follow the Jewish law in the matter of scourging. The Jews had an ancient law prohibiting more than forty lashes. The Pharisees, always making sure that the law was strictly kept, insisted that only thirty-nine lashes be given. In case of a miscount, they were sure of remaining within the law.

Preparations for Jesus' scourging were carried out according to Roman orders. The prisoner was stripped of his clothing and his hands tied to a post above his head. A Roman soldier stepped forward with the flagrum in his hand. This was a short whip consisting of several heavy, leather thongs with two small balls of lead attached near the ends of each. The heavy whip was brought down at full force again and again across Jesus' shoulders, back, and legs. At first, the weighted thongs cut through the skin only. Then, as the blows continued, they cut deep beneath the skin tissues, producing first an oozing of blood from the capillaries and veins of the skin and finally spurting arterial bleeding from vessels in the underlying muscles.

The small balls of lead first produced large deep bruises, which were broken open by subsequent blows. Finally, the skin of the back was hanging in long ribbons, and the entire area was an unrecognizable mass of torn, bleeding tissue. When it was determined by the centurion in charge that the prisoner was near death, the beating was finally stopped.

Mockery

The near-fainting Jesus was then untied and allowed to slump to the stone pavement, wet with His own blood. The Roman soldiers saw a great joke in this local Jew claiming to be a king. They threw a robe across His shoulders and placed a stick in His hand for a scepter. They still needed a crown to make their travesty complete. Small flexible branches covered with long thorns, commonly used to kindle fires in the courtyard, were plaited into the shape of a crude crown. The crown was pressed into His scalp and again there was much bleeding as the thorns pierced the very vascular tissue. After mocking Him and striking Him across the face, the soldiers took the stick from His hand and struck Him across the head, driving the thorns deeper into His scalp. Finally, they tired of their sadistic sport and tore the robe from His back. The robe had already become adherent to the clots of blood and serum in the wounds, and its removal, just as in the careless removal of surgical bandage, caused excruciating pain. The wounds began again to bleed.

Golgotha

In deference to Jewish custom, the Romans apparently returned His garments. The heavy patibulum of the cross was tied across His shoulders. The procession of the condemned Christ, two thieves, and the execution detail of Roman soldiers headed by a centurion began its slow journey along the route, which we know today as the Via Dolorosa.

In spite of Jesus' efforts to walk erect, the weight of the heavy wooden beam, together with the shock produced by much loss of blood, was too much. The rough beam of the wood gouged into the lacerated skin and muscles of the shoulders. The centurion, anxious to proceed with the crucifixion, selected a North African onlooker, Simon of Cyrene, to carry the cross. Jesus followed, still bleeding and sweating the cold, clammy sweat of shock. The estimated 650-yard journey to Golgotha was finally completed. The prisoner was again stripped of his clothing except for a loin cloth, which was allowed the Jews criminals being crucified.

The crucifixion began. Jesus was offered wine mixed with myrrh, and a mild analgesic, pain-relieving mixture. He refused the drink. Simon was ordered to place the patibulum on the ground, and Jesus was quickly thrown backward, with His shoulders against the wood. The soldier felt for the depression at the front of the wrist. He drove a heavy, square wrought-iron nail through the wrist and deep into the wood. Quickly, he moved to the other side and repeated the action, being careful not to pull the arms too tightly, but to allow some flexing and movement. The patibulum was then lifted into place at the top on the main stalk, and the title reading, "Jesus of Nazareth, King of the Jews" was nailed into place.

The left foot was pressed backward against the right foot. With both feet extended, toes down. A nail was driven through the arch of each, leaving the knees moderately flexed. The victim was now crucified.

On the Cross
As Jesus slowly sagged down with more weight on the nails in the wrists, excruciating, fiery pain shot along the fingers and up the arms to explode in the brain. The nails in the wrists were putting pressure on the large nerve trunks, which traverse the mid-wrist, and hand. As He pushed Himself upward to avoid this stretching torment, He placed His full weight on the nail through His feet. Again, there was searing agony as the nail tore through the nerves between the bones of the feet.

At this point another phenomenon occurred. As the arms fatigued, great waves of cramps swept over the muscles, knotting them in deep relentless, throbbing pain. With these cramps came the inability to push Himself upward. Hanging by the arms, the pectoral muscles of the chest, were paralyzed and the intercostal muscles, the small muscles between the ribs, were unable to act. Air could be drawn into the lungs, but could not be exhaled. Jesus fought to raise Himself in order to get even one short breath. Finally, the carbon dioxide level increased in the lungs and in the blood stream, and the cramps partially subsided.

The Last Words
Spasmodically, He was able to push Himself upward to exhale and bring in life-giving oxygen. It was undoubtedly during these periods that He uttered the seven short sentences which scripture records.

The first, looking down at the Roman soldiers throwing dice for His seamless garment: "Father, forgive them for they know not what they do."

The second, to the penitent thief: "Today, thou shalt be with Me in Paradise."
The third, looking down at Mary His mother, He said: "Woman, behold thy son." Then, turning to the terrified, grief-stricken adolescent John, the beloved apostle, He said, "Behold thy mother."

His fourth cry is from the beginning of Psalm 22: "My God, My God, why hast thou forsaken Me?"

He suffered hours of limitless pain, cycles of twisting, joint-rending cramps, intermittent partial asphyxiation, and searing pain as tissue was torn from His lacerated back from His movement up and down against the rough timbers of the cross. Then another agony began, a deep crushing pain in the chest as the sac surrounding the heart slowly filled with serum and began to compress the heart.

The prophecy in Psalm 22:14 was fulfilled: "I am poured out like water, and all my bones are out of joint, my heart is like wax; it is melted in the midst of my bowels."

The end was rapidly approaching. The loss of tissue fluids had reached a critical level; the compressed heart was struggling to pump heavy, thick, sluggish blood to the tissues, and the tortured lungs were making a frantic effect to inhale small gulps of air. The markedly dehydrated tissues sent their flood of stimuli to the brain. Jesus gasped His fifth cry: "I thirst." Again, we read in the prophetic psalm: "My strength is dried up like a potsherd; and my tongue cleaveth to my jaws; and thou has brought me into the dust of death."

A sponge soaked in the cheap sour wine, which was the staple drink of the Roman soldier, was put to Jesus' lips. His body was now in extremis, and He could feel the chill of death creeping through His tissues. This realization brought forth His sixth statement possibly little more than a tortured whisper: "It is finished." His mission of atonement had been completed. Finally, He could allow His body to die. With one last surge of strength, He once again pressed His torn feet against the nail, straightened His legs, took a deeper breath, and uttered His seventh and last cry: "Father, into thy hands I commit my spirit."

Death

We are all familiar with the final details of Jesus' execution. In order that the Sabbath not be profaned, the Jews asked that the condemned men be removed from their crosses. The common method of ending a crucifixion was by breaking the bones of the legs. This prevented the victim from pushing himself upward; the tension could not be relieved from the muscles of the chest, and rapid suffocation occurred. The legs of the two thieves were broken, but when the soldiers approached Jesus, they saw that this was not necessary.

Apparently, to make doubly sure of death, a soldier drove his lance between the ribs, upward through the tissues into the heart. John 19:34 states, "And immediately there came out blood and water." Thus, there was an escape of watery fluid from the sac surrounding His heart and the blood of the interior of the heart.

Resurrection
However, the crucifixion was not the end of the story. How grateful we are to have a glimpse of the infinite mercy of God toward man, the gift of atonement, the miracle of resurrection, and the expectation of Easter morning.

NOTE: the Arizona Medical Association originally published this article in Arizona Medicine in 1965. Dr. C. Truman Davis was a graduate of the University Of Tennessee College Of Medicine.
He practiced ophthalmology for twenty-four years. His widow has given permission to reproduce this article.

END-TIME STRATEGY

Daniel 7:25 He shall speak words against the Most High and shall <u>wear out</u> the saints of the Most High ...

Some commentators feel this scripture speaks of saints being worn out through persecution prior to the coming of the Lord. However, for the purpose of this lesson, we'll consider another application.

Saints distracted by worldly pursuits can become worn out saints. Saints doing the work of the ministry can also become worn out saints. Spiritual fatigue is, well, very fatiguing and can cause saints to be worn out.

Luke 21:34-36 And <u>take heed to yourselves</u>, lest at any time your hearts be overcharged with <u>surfeiting</u> and drunkenness, and cares of this life, and so that day come upon you unawares. For like a snare it shall come upon all them that dwell on the face of the whole earth. Watch ye, therefore, and pray always, that ye may be counted worthy to escape all these things that shall come to pass, and to stand before the Son of man.

Surfeiting is a Greek word (#2897) meaning, "headaches caused by excess." Some hearts are overcharged by surfing the World Wide Web. Others are overcharged by overcharging on credit cards and are then overcome by the cares of this world.

Luke chose the comparative word "like" to cause the reader to form a picture in his mind. He wrote, "like a snare." An animal caught in a snare will do anything to escape – including gnawing its foot off. Being caught in a snare is a desperate life and death struggle. Luke knew the reader would understand the implication.

Proverbs 1:17 Surely in vain the net (snare) is spread in the sight of any bird.

It's been said that birds are eyes with wings; meaning their wide range peripheral vision provides the keen awareness they need to survive as their wings offer a way of escape. Christians who pray to have the sight of a bird avoid hurtful snares. (Ask me how I know).

If we lose the vision of God's holiness, we have little hope of finishing the race set before us. And, if we lose sight of the goal of living a life acceptable to God, we will lose out of entering the eternal glory.

****

John Cochran wrote the following concerning Florence Chadwick, a long-distance swimmer born in San Diego in 1918.

It was a fog-shrouded morning, July 4, 1952, when a young woman named Florence Chadwick waded into the water off Catalina Island. She intended to be the first woman to swim the twenty-one miles from the island to the California coast. Long-distance swimming was not new to her; she had been the first woman to swim the English Channel in both directions.

The water was numbing cold that day. The fog was so thick she could hardly see the boats in her party. Several times sharks had to be driven away with rifle fire. She swam more than fifteen hours before she asked to be taken out of the water. Her trainer tried to encourage her to swim since they were so close to land, but when Florence looked, all she saw was fog. So she quit less than one-mile from her goal.

Later she said, "I'm not excusing myself, but if I could have seen the land I might have made it." It wasn't the cold or fear or exhaustion that caused Florence Chadwick to fail. It was the fog.

Two months later, Florence Chadwick walked off the same beach into the same channel and swam the distance, setting a new speed record, because she could see the land.

You are a long-distance saint who is accompanied by a trainer (the Holy Ghost) who sees beyond the fog and who knows the distance to the shoreline. You may be navigating through fog-shrouded shark-infested waters and you may be less than a mile from the shore!

Hebrews 12:1 Wherefore, seeing we also are compassed about with so great a cloud of witnesses, let us lay aside every weight, and the sin which doth so easily beset us, and let us run with patience the race that is set before us.

If you could see the size of the blessing coming and the eternal reward awaiting, you would understand the importance of the magnitude of the battle you are waging. When you stand before Jesus (the Judge), you will know He has depended on you in battles you weren't aware of. Until then, God's wisdom is for His saints to rest in Him while preserving in true faith.

FATHER, GIVE ME
FATHER, FORGIVE ME
FATHER, FORGIVE THEM

Bible parables are vivid metaphors which speak of common things experienced in life. Most do not have an obvious meaning. That's one reason why, when studying our Bible, we must be careful that we "dig out of it" and not "read into it."

Bible parables are designed to cause us to think (ponder) and to reason. They are open-ended leaving the reader to draw his own conclusion.

The Gospel of Luke, written by the only Gentile New Testament writer, has more parables than the other gospels. And only Luke's narrative teaches the parable of the lost son. This allegory, known as the "Prodigal Son" parable, is one the Bible's longest and most detailed parables, as well as one of the most loved.

In the beginning verse of **Luke 15** Jesus was speaking to tax collectors and sinners when Pharisees challenged Him by saying, "This man receiveth sinners, and eateth with them." He answered by speaking three parables: the lost sheep, the lost coin, and the lost son. In each of these three parables spoken to the Pharisees, all that had been lost was found. In the parable of the lost son, the father received his repentant son and ate with him, which directly contradicted the Pharisees murmuring against him for doing the same.

(Continued)
Parable of the Lost Son

Luke 15:11-12 And he (Jesus) said, A certain man had two sons; And the younger of them said to his father, Father, give me the portion of goods that falleth to me. And he divided unto them his living.

Though only the younger son asked for his inheritance, both sons would have been given what would have been their portion upon their father's death according to Jewish tradition.

We are not told that the father was astonished at such a brazen request; only that the petition was granted without debate. The father did not argue or intervene in his youngest son's free-will choice, just as God doesn't ours. God will merely step aside and allow us to continue in willful disobedience if we so choose.

15:13 And not many days after that, the younger son gathered all together, and took his journey into a far country, and there wasted his substance with riotous living.

The morally untethered younger son departed taking all his belongings expecting never to return. He didn't just pack for a weekend excursion into debauchery; he purposefully departed intending to immerse himself in sinful pleasures.

He reached the far country of his intended destination and wasted no time in wasting what had been bestowed by his father. The inheritance had not been earned; it was freely given. This son didn't go to the far country to seek a trade or other worthwhile pursuit. The thought of disgracing his family did not enter his lust-driven quest.

Among the many nuggets nestled within Proverbs is the following:

Proverbs 29:3 Whosoever loveth wisdom rejoiceth his father, but he that keepeth company with harlots spendeth his substance.

Proverbs 20:21 An inheritance may be gotten hastily at the beginning; but the end thereof shall not be blessed.

And here's a gem from the Psalms:

Psalm 119:9 Wherewithal shall a young man cleanse his way? By taking heed thereto according to thy word.

Thank God for His word and His Spirit given to guide us through life's maze!

The prodigal's saga continued with:

15:14 And when he had spent all, there arose a mighty famine in that land; and he began to be in want.

For the first time in his life, he experienced want (or need). This far country was not the utopia he had imagined. Perhaps, because of shame, he wasn't quite ready to begin the journey home.

15:15 And he went and joined himself to a citizen of that country; and he sent him into his fields to feed swine.

The thought of this son feeding swine added to the drama of the parable since the listening Pharisees well knew that Levitical Law **(Leviticus 11:7-8)** forbid Jews from touching swine. Their hearts and minds must have filled with contempt as they intently listened.

15:16 And he would fain (gladly) have filled his belly with the husks that the swine did eat; and no man gave unto him.

The lost son experienced degrading disillusionment in the quagmire of despair while no one offered assistance. That was a horrible place to be in, my friend. And yet oftentimes that is the place we find ourselves in until we seek the Lord and His mercy. How many times have we thought when observing tragedies all around us, "There, but for the grace of God, go I."

15:17-19 And when he came to himself, he said, How many of my father's servants have bread enough and to spare, and I perish with hunger! I will arise and go to my father, and will say unto him, Father I have sinned against heaven, and before thee, and am no more worthy to be called thy son; make me as one of thy hired servants.

The first sentence of these verses contains the only exclamation mark in the entire story! Now we're getting to the crux of the matter. The son has had a talk with himself and formulated a plan to escape the famine. He had reached the bottom and had started looking up. There's nothing like a trip down Memory Lane to create a longing deep within our hearts. He remembered the good things at his father's house and knew that everyone there had their needs met with plenty to spare.

In **John 14:2**, Jesus referred to heaven as His Father's house. And, you know, there's room for all in the Father's house.

Proverbs 9:12 If thou be wise, thou shalt be wise for thyself; but if thou scoffest (scornest), thou alone shalt bear it.

This wayward son now knew what it was to be lost and alone bearing the burden of his unwise choices. It's commendable that he accepted full responsibility without blaming others. Sounds like he may have matured as he bumped along. With the loss of all his material goods, his load had been lightened for the trek home. But now he carried the heavier burden of sin.

He devised a well-scripted plan to recite when approaching his forsaken-father who immediately spoke with an unscripted from-the-heart response. This presented to the Pharisees a perfect allegory of God's redemptive love.

The next few verses deserve careful examination as they add a poignant crescendo. The son arrived home unannounced expecting only to utter his well-rehearsed plea. What occurred was a breath-taking exchange between the merciful father and his repentant son.

15:20 And he arose, and came to his father. But when he was yet a great way off, his father saw him, and had compassion, and ran, and fell on his neck, and kissed him.

That little word, "But" might be one of the biggest little words in the Bible. "But when he was yet a great way off, his father saw him ..." Why did his father see him when he was yet a great way off? Because he was watching daily eagerly hoping for his return at any moment, my friend; just as God waits for His own.

Many times I have earnestly prayed for sinners and backsliders pleading that they were "so far out there – they are just so way off!" And, they were from my point of view but not from God's. He is watching and sees them coming home when they are "yet a great way off." Are those whom you are praying for "yet a great way off"? Rest assured that the unseen hand of our God is working in far above ways to gather them unto Himself.

Then his father, "saw him, and had compassion, and ran, and fell on his neck, and kissed him." My, my, what a greeting; what a reunion! The action of his father far exceeded the hope of the contrite son keenly aware of his unworthiness.

Surely this vividly told scenario impacted the Pharisees who had knowledge of the Law of Moses without knowing the merciful law-giver. And, what about the tax collectors and sinners who were standing near and had lived all their lives under the yoke of religion without mercy?

15:21 And the son said unto him, Father, I have sinned against heaven, and in thy sight, and am no more worthy to be called thy son.

He humbly acknowledged his grievous sins before God and before his father. By saying he was no more worthy to be called his son, he accepted that he had no hope of restoration. He was willing to do whatever his father required, just as we need to be.

The father never answered his son; his actions spoke louder than words. Without reprimanding his son, the father gave directions to his hired servants.

15:22-23 But the father said to his servants, Bring forth the best robe, and put it on him; and put a ring on his hand, and shoes on his feet. And bring the fatted calf, and kill it; and let us eat, and be merry.

The bestowed gifts distinguished this fully pardoned son from the hired servants. The best robe was a full-length robe of dignity and status. The ring demonstrated his restored authority within his father's household. The shoes (or sandals) showed that he was not a servant but a son, as servants did not wear shoes.

Then the father told his servants:

15:24 For this, my son, was dead, and is alive again; he was lost, and is found. And they began to be merry.

The father gladly received him as "my son" whereas the son had been afraid to ask to be called his son.

In the two preceding parables of this chapter (the parable of the lost sheep and the parable of the lost coin), that which was lost had been sought and found. Not so with the lost son. He had to come to himself (recognized his hopeless, helpless condition) and choose to seek forgiveness, just as we must.

Notice the change in verb tense: was dead/is alive, was lost/is found. The father's gracious greeting evidenced his eagerness. My friend, throughout history, those who followed false "little g gods" have <u>never</u> been offered reconciliation. Reconciliation is a glorious gift!

Jesus, the perfect sinless Lamb of God, made peace between sinners and God:
    Ephesians 2:16 And that he might reconcile both unto God in one body by the cross ...

Luke 15:25-28 Now his elder son was in the field; and as he came and drew nigh (near) to the house, he heard music and dancing. And he called one of the servants, and asked what these things meant. And he said unto him, Thy brother is come; and thy father hath killed the fatted calf, because he hath received him safe and sound. And he was angry, and would not go in; therefore came his father out, and entreated him.

The elder son had industriously worked in his father's field. It's curious that the father had not sent him word to come and receive his brother and to join in the rejoicing. Because of anger, he did not rejoice when his father's heart overflowed with joy.

Jealously can be ignited by a self-righteous spirit. The elder brother represented the Pharisees, who were self-righteous and indifferent toward repentant sinners. The expression "safe and sound" is only used here in the Bible. The servant may have meant the son was now <u>safe</u> from the evil world and of a <u>sound</u> or healthy mind and heart.

The father had run to meet the returning son, he then came to "entreat" the angry son. Entreat is a Greek (#3870) word meaning "invite, beseech."

The angry elder son responded to his father's request:
15:29 And, he, answering, said to his father, Lo these many years do I serve thee, neither transgressed I at any time thy commandment; and yet thou never gavest me a kid, that I might make merry with my friends.

Like the Pharisees, who had kept the letter of the law, the elder son felt jealous and angry that his sinning brother had been received. His anger fueled-jealousy caused him to say "thou never gavest me a kid." Anger and bitterness over-ruled appreciation for his double portion inheritance. When someone is bitter, my friend, they just can't see the blessing. Circumstance can expose the raw nerves of long-standing resentment. Hurt feelings can be the reflex of built-up emotions like time-released damage from the past.

The elder son did not know what he would encounter on this day. Just as our lives unfold day-by-day, so did his. We need to be alert and prayerfully prepared, dear one, for each new day.

15:30 But as soon as this, thy son, was come, who hath devoured thy living with harlots, thou hast killed for him the fatted calf.

The elder son did not acknowledge the younger son as his brother; only as "thy son." We aren't told that the elder son even greeted the returning and repentant brother.

15:31-32 And he said unto him, Son, thou art ever with me, and all I have is thine. It was fitting that we should make merry, and be glad; for this, thy brother, was dead, and is alive again; and was lost, and is found.

The elder son was compassionately scolded without condemnation. The repentant son was compassionately restored without being scolded. The older son represents the law with its demand for justice; whereas the younger son, represents the saving grace bestowed upon repentant sinners at the cross.

I can appreciate that the father bestowed Christ-like mercy of each son, but I cannot comprehend the mercy of God toward His children. Let's just say, I'm not there yet.

Jesus taught this parable as He journeyed to His appointment in Jerusalem. It could well be that these same Pharisees, tax collectors, and sinners were in Jerusalem for the Passover at the time of His public humiliation and crucifixion. Perhaps they heard the first words He spoke while impaled on the cross.

Jesus prayed while suffering unimaginable agony:
Luke 23:34 Then Jesus said, Father, forgive them, for they know not what they do.

The son implored, Father, give me

He later pleaded, Father, forgive me

Jesus the Son prayed, Father, forgive them

... HOW GREAT IS THAT DARKNESS

University of California-Berkeley Professor Timothy Leary was often in the news during the 1960's. He was known as the father of LSD and devoted his life to promoting its use. The most powerful hallucinogenic drug, LSD produces a psychedelic state where the user is detached from reality. Professor Leary believed using LSD was a normal pursuit of happiness.

During the era of this drug culture, over 3,000,000 Americans between twelve and twenty-five years of age, used LSD and became known as the acidhead generation. It wreaked havoc in their lives which many times resulted in their death. After taking LSD, the user was said to be "on a trip." Professor Leary took his final trip at age seventy-six.

In his final years, when stricken with cancer, the professor became re-occupied with planning his death. While on his deathbed, he asked to be carried outside to watch an expected celestial event. As a shooting star streaked across the night sky, he pointed to it and exclaimed, "I am that star!" The star quickly burned out.

During his lifetime, he identified himself as a pagan.

John 3:19 And this is the condemnation, that light is come into the world, and men loved darkness rather than light, because their deeds were evil.

Matthew 6:23 ... If, therefore, the light that is in thee be darkness, how great is that darkness!

John 8:12 I am the light of the world; he that followeth me shall not walk in darkness, but shall have the light of life.

In the only psalm attributed to Moses, we are instructed by his prayerful words:

Psalm 90:9,10,12 ... we spend our years as a tale that is told. The days of our years are three-score and ten; and if, by reason of strength, they be fourscore years, yet is their strength labor and sorrow; for it is soon cut off, and we fly away. So teach us to number our days, that we may apply our hearts unto wisdom.

Processor Leary lived a total of 27,555 days.

Timothy Leary   B: 10-22-1920   D: 03-31-1996

I HAVE ALLOWED THIS

Perhaps this is another testimony that should be under the heading, "Some Things Just Won't Preach." My writing about such things may be fueled by a desire to truly walk with God allowing Him to teach me truths along the way. A "religious mindset" can be rigid to the point of shuttering our minds and hearts. So, my prayer is that He make me teachable.

Here's a favorite scripture that I pray often:

3rd John :4 I have no greater joy than to hear that my children walk in truth.

The following was told by Brother Thomas, an associate pastor of our church. It's an unvarnished account from the lips of a weary man who had tried everything he knew to help Marsha, a church member who suffering from mental illness.

Brother Thomas said he couldn't recall the number of times his phone rang well into the night with someone seeking help for Marsha. He would dubitably go to her hospital bedside, sit, and listen while feeling like an armchair annalist. It was as though she was marooned in a delusional world all her own. She would seldom regain mental equilibrium between reeling episodes of confusion.

This was especially perplexing to Brother Thomas because he knew God, knew the power of prayer and understood that demonic forces had ensnared Marsha. Sitting at her bedside one evening, he prayed imploring the Lord to allow him to understand why He had not delivered her.

The answer he received wasn't what he expected:

"I have allowed this so she would serve me."

It was startling. God gave no additional explanation. He is God; He doesn't need to explain. As the years have gone by, Marsha has gained a good measure of stability and has demonstrated a true love for God. A son was faithful to drive her to church services and would usually wait in his car for service to end. Gradually, and I do mean gradually, this son would sit with her during the services. God was working.

Then came the day. There they were - Marsha, her sons, her daughters-in-law, and a grandson holding hands and praying in a circle at the altar. Their physical family had become a spiritual family united in Christ through her efforts and those of fellow church members. Marsha and her family remain today as a united family in Christ. To God be the glory!

Romans 11:33 Oh, the depth of the riches both of the wisdom and knowledge of God! How unsearchable are his judgments, and his ways are past finding out!

I LEFT OFF DEALING WITH HER
FIFTY YEARS AGO

On an ordinary day as I was doing household chores an unexpected new reality jolted my heart and forever crimped my theology as I prayed a simple prayer. I had been disturbed by our great-aunt Marie's adamant rejection of God. Even the mention of the name of Jesus over-loaded her tolerance level.

When Marie was eight years old, she and her siblings had been orphaned by a train accident that caused the tragic death of both their parents in 1928. Marie and her siblings were then raised in a Birmingham, Alabama orphanage.

Even before World War II began in 1939, young Marie had found her way to Washington, D.C. where she began a long-lasting career with the Federal government. After working many years, the self-made never-married Marie retired with a comfortable income. For reasons known only to God and Marie, she had hardened her heart like the hide of a rhino; she wanted nothing to do with Him –
F I N A L!

Even knowing her hardened heart, I was still concerned for her soul. And, knowing that our Father God is merciful beyond our ability to comprehend, I prayed a simple prayer, "Lord, Aunt Marie is ninety-four now. Please don't let her slip between the cracks." His immediate response came as a jolt that crimped my theology, "I left off dealing with her fifty years ago!" Until that moment I had believed, "Where there's breath, there's hope." However, the instant He spoke that thought vanished. I dared not utter a word. His declaration of rejecting Marie was as adamant as her in rejecting Him. It was absolute. It was awful. So, without Marie knowing or caring, she had been a "dead man walking" for fifty years.

God had known Marie's heart throughout her lifetime. He didn't interfere or override her personal choices, just as He doesn't ours. He even allowed her to live years beyond the ordinary "expiration date." The fact is God is not fair, God is not equal, but God is absolutely just.

1st Corinthians 8:3 But if any man love God, the same is known of him.

And, conversely, God also knows those who don't.

IN HONOR OF GENEVA MARTIN
AND HER GOD

Consideration was given to naming this, "Somethings Just Won't Preach," as I had mentioned regarding another earlier story. Even though I wrote it like it happened, it may rumple some readers.

It's now been years, but the vivid memory lingers. I was standing by my husband on the platform after the close of a Sunday evening service when I noticed Geneva standing praying pleading in deep distress at the altar. Other seekers were praying but the depth of her despair griped my soul. The Lord let me know that she was praying wrong. Yes, that's right; praying wrong.

Without forethought, I bolted from the platform with an urgency I hadn't felt before or since. I had to stop her. I stood before her with my hands on her shoulders, and the words I spoke surprised me but they didn't seem to surprise her. It may have been that her brokenness was an open door to receive God's counsel. I shared, "Geneva, the Lord said you were praying wrong." His peace settled on us both. I continued, "Let's stand here and pray; perhaps He'll show us how to pray." I had no idea what she had been praying about and was not prepared when He disclosed, "CANCER. I have undertaken for her; before she knew about it, I have undertaken."

I didn't have liberty to share this revelation with her at that time. I was to learn that Geneva had been aware of a lump in her breast for two years. Her life was full of helping establish the church, teaching Sunday school, working with her husband, and running her home. That was more than enough for this sixty-eight year old grandmother who didn't want to take time to investigate an ominous lump. At the urging of her husband, she sought medical counsel. After a few weeks, she received the diagnosis: Stage 4 Cancer.

People who don't know the Lord or who don't trust Him view "The Big C" as cancer. Whereas, believers know The Big C is Christ. Geneva knew and trusted The Big C. Yes, she went to this doctor, that doctor, this hospital, and that hospital; but her faith was in God alone. She became weary but not shaken. She truly glorified her Savior through it all.

Geneva suffered during the passing months, as I kept thinking; He said He had undertaken. That must mean we don't need an undertaker, right? (Wrong)

When I glanced at her during a worship service, the Lord explained, "I am honoring her in this."

1st Peter 4:19 Wherefore, let them that suffer according to the will of God commit the keeping of their souls to him in well-doing, as unto a faithful Creator.

The capitol "C" used for Creator make it a proper noun; meaning a specific person. The Creator knows what He is creating through what we call suffering. When we are suffering, we are to commit ourselves to a faithful Creator; not to a faithful deliverer or a faithful defender, even though He is those things too.

Romans 8:18 For I reckon that the sufferings of this present time are not worthy to be compared with the glory that shall be revealed in us.

John 21:19 This spoke he (Jesus), signifying by what death he should glorify God.

Yes, dear saints, God desires that He be glorified in our deaths. Geneva walked all the way with God; all the way to the glory world and into His outstretched arms.

Geneva Jones Martin

Born: 09-12-1939   Died: 04-30-2001

Philippians 2:21 For to me to live is Christ, and to die is gain.

IT WAS A SERIOUS NON-ISSUE ISSUE

This account has circled the globe more than once and has now surprisingly landed on your lap. It's about a non-issue doing its best to bloom into a serious issue.

Newlyweds, Adrian and Camila encountered something they disagreed about. It may have remained minute or dissolved altogether had Camila not been quite so inflexible. She was determined to "stand her ground" so to speak.

Adrian was accustomed to shedding his jacket and work clothes by placing them across their bed at the end of the day. This practice was entirely unacceptable to Camila who had set a nonnegotiable boundary: there would be NO clothing placed on their bed. For Adrian, this was an absurd requirement. Adrian wanted to know, indeed, needed to know why. Camila's response was as puzzling as her "no clothing on the bed" policy. As if it would end all strife, she exclaimed, "Because my mother said so!" Since she had never questioned whatever her mother said, she wasn't able to give any reason for the passed down rule.

Adrian knew there had to be a reason – a valid reason. A quick call to his mother-in-law made this issue a non-issue. When asked, his mother-in-law had to pause to even remember this rule, "Oh, I know what it was. The neighbors' children had head lice. I didn't want any of their clothing put on anything in the house – much less a bed." Adrian's communication with her was brief but provided that one little bit of understanding that insured the would-be issue would forever be a non-issue.

There's nothing like communication to bring clarity and understanding. Those who are earnestly endeavoring to understand God are praying (communicating) to Him. When understanding of God and His word seeps into our hearts, it comes like a healing balm. Whereas, not understanding God creates fertile ground within our hearts for layered acres of anger, hurt, bitterness, and resentment. Through not communicating with the Lord, things that are actually non-issues can rapidly become insurmountable issues.

It's become common today to hear, "He's got issues," or some such statement; meaning there are problems or people in this person's life that are conflicting.

The word "keep" in **Proverbs 4:23** conveys a powerful directive. Keep is a Hebrew word (#5341) which means, "guard, protect, maintain."

Proverbs 4:23 Keep thy heart with all diligence; for out of it are the issues of life.

Detrimental life altering issues can be avoided when we keep our own hearts. Guarding our heart is certainly worth the effort when we realize that our "issues" can be past to the next generation and even beyond.

I'VE KILLED THOUSANDS

Minutes before being taken out by a police sharp-shooter positioned on the rooftop of a nearby post office, Oliver Huberty was said to have boasted, "I've killed thousands, and I'll kill thousands more."

This incomprehensibly horrific scene took place July 18, 1984 at a McDonald's restaurant in San Ysidro, California. Twenty-one people were massacred and fifteen injured. Huberty killed employees and customers using a Uzi submachine gun. Everyone was a target from an eight-month-old baby to a seventy-four-year-old man. He never intended to take hostages. Some hunkered down under tables, but to no avail.

Oliver Huberty's home contained an arsenal of weapons. Two days before the massacre he told his wife that he thought he was having a mental problem. Later he called a mental health facility and asked for an appointment. The clerk, not sensing an urgency in his voice, listed his request as "non-urgent."

An hour later, he kissed his wife good-bye. She asked where he was going. "I'm going to hunt humans," was all the forty-one year old said before walking 200 yards to their neighborhood McDonald's.

Oliver Huberty didn't have a military background, so there's little chance that he had killed thousands. Perhaps it wasn't Olive Huberty who made the boast.

John 8:44 ... (Jesus speaking of Satan) He was a murderer from the beginning.

Scripture gives us the progression in:

Mark 7:21-23 For from within, out of the heart of men, proceed evil thoughts, adulteries, fornications, murders, thefts, covetousness, wickedness, deceit, lasciviousness (evil desire), and evil eye, blasphemy, pride, foolishness. All these evil things come from within and defile the man.

Oliver Huberty had told his wife that he thought he was having a mental problem. He was. His thoughts then became actions. The spirit(s) who occupied Oliver Huberty are still actively occupying others today.

The nobleman in Luke's parable gave his servants abilities; then clear instructions to:

Luke 19:13 ... occupy til I come.

Jesus won the victory but we must enforce it until He comes. The five-inch space between our ears is the territory that needs to be occupied more than any other. Occupying that space can be an on-going challenge.

2nd Corinthians 10:5 Casting down imaginations, and every high thing that exalteth itself against the knowledge of God, and bringing into captivity every thought to the obedience of Christ ...

James 4:7 Submit yourselves therefore unto God. Resist the devil, and he will flee from you.

A satisfying victorious life awaits those who submit to God and then resist the devil and see him flee as the defeated foe he is. We are to occupy til He comes!

KNOWLEDGE FALSELY SO CALLED

Not every person's life-after-death experience is the real deal. I listened sadly as a woman told of her afterlife experience. During her experience, an "angel" had stressed that acquiring knowledge was the most important thing in this life. My heart throbbed when she said she had received this all-important truth. There was no mention of Jesus, holiness, or the kingdom of God in her afterlife experience.

This poor deceived woman returned to her body with a consuming zeal to learn anything and everything. Within ten years she had earned three undergraduate degrees and was then working on a Master's degree in chemistry. She stated that even with all of this accumulation of knowledge, she was not satisfied. No one could persuade her that her afterlife experience was false. There's no telling where her pursuit has led, but I dare say it wasn't to the love of the truth. It could be that she has by now "died by degrees."

Paul cautioned young Timothy to avoid profane and vain babblings and oppositions of knowledge falsely so called. **(1nd Timothy 6:2)**

Hosea 4:6 My people are destroyed for lack of knowledge; because thou hast rejected knowledge, I will also reject thee ...

Notice that the people had rejected the knowledge of God. It wasn't that they didn't have opportunity to know Him.

2nd Peter 2:20 tells us that we escape the pollutions of the world through the knowledge of the Lord and Savior, Jesus Christ.

You may recall the children's beginner books of years ago; books like the Little Golden Books for Kids series. How we struggled to learn the letters and to read those preprimary little books. With our first moment in the glory world, we'll understand that the Bible was our preprimary book during our lifetime. When launched into eternity, we'll enter the realm of ever-expanding knowledge and adoration of God.

2nd Peter 1:2 Grace and peace be multiplied to you through the knowledge of God, and of Jesus, our Lord …

1st Peter 1:21 Who by him (Jesus) do believe in God, who raised him up from the dead and gave him glory, that your faith and hope might be in God.

Romans 12:3 … God has dealth to every man a measure of faith.

2nd Corinthians 13:5 Examine yourselves, whether ye be in the faith; prove your own selves.

It is your duty to make sure your faith is in the true and living God. Keep in mind that God is not who you think He is. He is who He says He is.

LOOK WHAT GOD GAVE

God gave:

Noah a boat	Abraham a promise
Jacob a ladder	Joseph a robe
Moses a rod	Joshua a shout
Gideon a sword	David a stone

He gave us a name

Isaiah 9:6 For unto us a child is born, unto us a son is given, and the government shall be upon his shoulder; and his name shall be called Wonderful, Counselor, The Mighty God, The Everlasting Father, The Prince of Peace.

John 3:16 For God so loved the world that he gave his only begotten Son, that whosoever believeth in him should not perish, but have everlasting life.

Acts 4:12 Neither is there salvation in any other; for there is no other name under heaven given among men, whereby we must be saved.

Keep in mind, dear saint:

Luke 12:48 ... For onto whom much is given, of him shall be required much ...

LORD, SAVE THESE GAMBLERS

Some churches no longer ask members to stand and testify. A pastor said it is because many tend to bog down in unrelated details rather than testifying about what the Lord had done for them. Their testifying is more like a ramble of, "I over-slept this morning and had to rush to get out the door headed to work. I backed over my neighbor's mailbox before hitting my garbage can. And, if that wasn't bad enough, I got a $200 speeding ticket even though I wasn't really speeding." The hearers of this type "testimony" are by then sighing an "Ahem," instead of a hardy, "Amen." Seldom is even a spark of God's Spirit transmitted to the congregation. Result: God is not glorified and the congregation is not edified.

Back when church testifying was really testifying, from time to time, our pastor would call out from the podium, "Brother John, stand and testify!" This routine request filled my heart with joyful anticipation even though Brother John had stood and shared the same testimony over and over. It had the same beginning, the same middle, and the same ending. Always predictable and yet I never tired of hearing it told; it blessed my soul.

There was no need to pass a microphone to Brother John. His deep baritone voice filled the sanctuary as he spoke this poignant testimony.

Harold, Sam, Ted, and he had been a bunch of sin-loving beer-drinking buddies who enjoyed a weekly poker game at John's house. John loved his wife, Ann, even though he didn't appreciate her Christian faith. He let it be known he didn't want to hear about all that "religious junk." Ann wisely relied on prayer and remained out of earshot of their joke telling laced with profanity and uproarious laughter coming from their enclosed patio.

Following Ann's death, John became a believer. He grieved over the years he wasted not loving God and not supporting his wife in her walk with the Lord. He lamented deeply over the lost opportunities of each of his buddies prior to their deaths. But he tearfully rejoiced when telling of the miracles done by the unseen hand of God that had converted each of them to the love of the truth. One by one they came as each followed a variety of paths that brought them to the foot of the Cross. Jesus covered them with His precious blood and changed them all from the inside out. They were, indeed, all made new.

Then came the day when John felt he needed to dismantle the old card table they had sat around those many years gambling away their lives. It was a bittersweet task. He folded the chairs stacking them neatly in a corner. When he turned the table over to remove its legs, he noticed a hand-written note taped underneath. It was a prayer Ann placed there years ago.

Ann had simply requested,

"Lord, save these gamblers."

MAN MADE TO WORSHIP

There has never been a dog that worshiped an ocean or a giraffe that worshiped the sun. Only man is known to worship both the ocean and the sun. Also, other animals are not aware of the passing of time as man is. Our Creator placed in us an awareness of the passing of time and an awareness of Him.

Ecclesiastes 3:11 He hath made everything beautiful in its time; also he hath set eternity in their heart ...

Archaeologists excavating extinct civilizations have discovered common elements existing at the time of their demise. Large sports arenas and worship involving human sacrifice were shared factors.

While driving home years ago, the Lord interjected in my vision a stainless steel pedestal. I knew instantly that it was a physician's examining table. I was struck by a horrible realization, "It's an abortion table!" God then added that it was an altar of sacrifice to the god of self.

This lesson will present an unusual approach to applying the verses in **2nd Thessalonians 2:3-12**.

The Apostle Paul wrote this 2nd epistle soon after writing his first letter to the church of Thessalonica in A.D. 51.

Its main purpose was to reassure the saints that the great tribulation time before the day of the Lord had not begun. His writing to correct this erroneous teaching has provided for us a clear expectation of events foretold in the Book of Revelation.

2nd Thessalonians 2:3-4 Let no man deceive you by any means; for that day shall not come, except there come a falling away first, and that man of sin be revealed, the son of perdition, who opposeth and exalteth himself above all that is called God, or that is worshiped, so that he, as God sitteth in the temple of God, showing himself that he is God.

Men can be deceived by themselves, by others, and/or by evil spirits. We live in a day when fallen-man sits on the throne of his own heart exalting himself as god. "The son of perdition" is opposing everything that is of God while he elevates or promotes himself. Perdition is a Greek word (#684) meaning, "destruction."

The prophet Isaiah revealed five self-exalting thoughts of Lucifer:

Isaiah 14:13-14 For thou hast said in thine heart, I will ascend into heaven, I will exalt my throne above the stars of God; I will sit upon the mount of the congregation, in the sides of the north, I will ascend above the heights of the clouds, I will be like the Most High.

He's doing that today by "sitting in the temple of God (man's heart), and showing himself that he is God."

The wrath of God is revealed from heaven against those: **Romans 1:25** Who changed the truth of God into a lie, and worshipped and served the creature more than the Creator, who is blessed forever. Amen.

Man was created by God to worship Him alone. He is certainly aware of those who are worshipping Him and those who are worshipping themselves.

MARGARET SAID IT WAS REAL

Margaret was accustomed to handling cash. Together with her husband and son, she had owned and operated successful businesses for many years.

I happened to be in her office when a strange looking and stranger feeling $100. bill was found in a stack of money to be deposited. It was thicker than the other currency. And, unlike the other, it was printed in bright colors. The woman preparing the bank deposit was suspicious. She said, "Look at this," as she handed it to Margaret who then twisted it this way and that way saying, "Yes, it's real." However, it looked to me like a rather bad forgery, so I chimed in, "Oh, no. That's not real. It's a counterfeit!" As an experienced money-handler, Margaret overrode my concerns. The counterfeit-looking bill was made a part of the deposit and was later accepted by the bank's teller without question.

Three natural senses (sight, smell, and touch) had deceived me. It appeared bogus, it smelled worse than the other currency, and it felt very coarse and crinkly. But I lacked the experience needed to discern between the real and unreal.

Discerning between real and unreal, between good and evil is a lifelong pursuit ordained by God for His children. Once we begin experiencing the true Spirit of God, we are able to detect the spiritual counterfeit (fake, false, phony) things that cross our paths.

1st Corinthians 2:14 But the natural man receiveth not the things of the Spirit of God; for they are foolishness unto him, neither can he know them because they are spiritually discerned.

Hebrews 5:14 But strong meat (solid food) belongeth to them that are of full age (mature), even those who by reason of use have their senses exercised to discern both good and evil.

Spiritual maturity should be a major goal of every Christian. Without spiritual discernment, we are feeble, ineffective wounded soldiers and become an easy prey.

2nd Corinthians 2:11 Lest Satan should get an advantage of us; for we are not ignorant of his devices.

Those who remain ignorant of his devices will also remain POWs in this war and will lose out on their eternal reward as well.

Ephesians 6:11 Put on the whole armor of God, that ye may be able to stand against the wiles of the devil.

The word "wiles" is a Greek word (#8180), meaning "method or trickery." How can anyone stand against "the wiles of the devil" if they are unaware of them?

Police study a criminal's mode of operating or method of working known as his "modus operandi." We know the modus operandi of Satan. The eighth chapter of the Gospel of John states that he is the father of lies and has been a murderer from the beginning. Tracking his activity is not difficult for those who spiritually discern.

An older pastor recently made a somewhat surprising statement, "You would not be worth much without the devil." Let's consider his statement. Without the adversary, we would remain ignorant of good and evil and less aware of right and wrong. We would never learn to resist evil and to choose the right. We would be of little value to our Almighty God.

1st John 4:1 Beloved, believe not every spirit, but try (Greek #1381 discern, prove) the spirits whether they are of God ...

And speaking of recognizing counterfeits, Jesus warned of the following:

Matthew 24:24 For there shall arise false Christs, and false prophets, and shall show great signs and wonders, insomuch that, if it were possible, they shall deceive the very elect.

Notice that this scripture says, "if it were possible." Those who try the spirits will not be deceived and ensnared by Satan.

OH, BOY, THAT'S MY KIND OF SCRIPTURE!

Carolyn spoke from her heart and didn't expect those within earshot to think her comment was comical. Her youthful yet beyond-plump appearance was something she could not hide. She quoted a portion of Paul's counsel written to Timothy, "for bodily exercise profiteth little," and gleefully exclaimed, "Oh, boy, that's my kind of scripture!"

Dear saints, as tempting as it would be to "read into" scriptures rather than to 'dig out of them," we should guard against reading and quoting partial verses, and applying them in whatever fashion we choose.

The scripture Carolyn quoted and misapplied comes from:

1st Timothy 4:7-8 But refuse profane and old wives' fables, and exercise thyself rather unto godliness. For bodily exercise profiteth little, but godliness is profitable unto all things, having promise of the life that now is, and of that which is to come.

Like you, I do not want to pervert the word of God, but to aid our understanding, I will take a little liberty here. Everyone who has experienced even brief sessions of deliberate physical exercise knows of its benefit. Our endurance escalates exponentially. In writing that "bodily exercise profiteth little," Paul may have been offering an analogy, such as bodily exercise profiteth little when compared to being exercised for godliness which will benefit us now and in the life to come.

Ecclesiastes 1:13 I gave my heart to seek and search out by wisdom concerning all things that are done under heaven; this sore (severe) travail hath God given to the sons of man to be exercised therewith.

It is indeed a sore travail to seek and search for God's wisdom while living in a corrupt world engulfed in evil.

Hebrews 12:11 Now no chastening for the present seemeth to be joyous, but grievous; nevertheless afterward it yieldeth the peaceable fruit of righteousness unto them which are exercised thereby.

Bad behavior is joyous to juveniles until they begin to suffer its consequences. As we begin to grow-up in God, we see and appreciate the benefits of His chastening.

Speaking of growing up, we cannot become mature sons of God, if we don't distinguish what is of God and what isn't; and that involves being exercised.

Hebrews 5:14 But strong meat belongeth to them that are of full age, even who by reason of their use have their senses exercised to discern both good and evil.

That one scripture lets us know that this boot camp is not for sissies, half-hearted, or lackadaisical would-be saints. Our earth journey is more like an elimination round doused with copious amounts of love, mercy, and grace.

Enjoy the challenge of your journey!

THE WORST ASSIGNMENT

There may be times when you feel your God-given assignment is too much; that it's an impossible mission. Should this happen, please consider the horrendous assignment given the two men chosen to care for the beaten, bloody, and dead body of our Lord Jesus Christ.

Scripture reveals that Joseph of Arimathaea was a rich man, a Sanhedrin member who had not consented to their counsel concerning Jesus **(Luke 23:51)**, was known as a righteous man and an honorable counselor **(Mark 15:43)**. Without thought of self-preservation, he went boldly and openly before Pilate and begged to be given His torn body. **(Matthew 27:57-58)** This courageous man knew Pilate could have said, "So, you were his disciple. Should I crucify you too?"

The Bible identifies Nicodemus as a Pharisee and a ruler of the Jews. We know that, because he feared other Jews, he had come to Jesus at night seeking to understand. The discourse between Jesus and Nicodemus **(John 3)** is the longest private instruction recorded as given by our Lord. This was an important conversation. All twenty-five scriptures recording Jesus having said, "Verily, verily" are found in the Gospel of John. Interestingly, three of the twenty-five were spoken directly to Nicodemus.

Later, Nicodemus quelled a dispute among other Pharisees concerning Jesus. **(John 7:51-53)** The actions of this chosen man following the Lord's humiliation, suffering, and death, showed he was unashamed to openly declare that this was indeed the Son of God.

Joseph of Arimathaea and Nicodemus had not fully known their assignment in advance. (And neither do you yours). Without their foreknowledge, they were chosen by God for the most horrific assignment in all of human history. God entrusted the body of His Son to their care. They literally took the cross down with Jesus still impaled. They removed His hands and feet from the spikes and then prepared His broken, bloodied, and bruised body for burial.

The grief-stricken dazed disciples had all fled. Jesus had told them twice in three scriptures: **(Matthew 20:19, 26:2, Mark 10:34)** that He would be crucified, yet the actual event was incomprehensible. These Jewish men had all worshiped Jesus and believed He was the promised Messiah; the Son of God. **(Matthew 14:33)** Were they wondering how they could have been so deceived as to trust that this crucified man was the Son of God? He had delegated authority to them to cast out demons, heal the sick, and preach the gospel. **(Mark 6:7-12 Luke 9:1, 10:19)** Yet, the reality of what they saw was a lifeless mutilated mass of ripped up flesh hanging helplessly. Did they feel the power He had delegated to them must have been a farce because what they saw did not meet their expectations? What went wrong?

According to Jewish law **(Deuteronomy 21:22-23)**, a criminal must be buried on the day he was hanged. The God-given task assigned to Joseph of Arimathaea and

Nicodemus had to be done; somebody had to do it. The evening had come and the Sabbath was approaching. Leaving His body impaled after dark would have increased the risk of further desecration, of its being stolen, or to possibly have become a prey of feral dogs.

Because he had not known what he would be required to do, Joseph of Arimathaea had not brought the linen burial cloth with him. Scripture says that rather than, "brought," that he actually "bought" the linen burial cloth. **(Mark 15:46)** He never thought that the tomb he purchased for his personal use would contain the body of the only begotten Son of God. **(Matthew 27:61)**

Nicodemus went to Golgotha expecting to care for the body of our Lord. He had brought nearly one hundred pounds of burial ointments. **(John 19:39)**

Once their sacred heart-wrenching duty was performed, these honorable men returned to their homes with heavy hearts but with clear consciences knowing they had done their best. The Thorn-crowned King had been laid to rest. Like each of us, these men had God-given free wills. They could have chosen to be sequestered in the comfort of their homes ignoring the call of God. As they approached His cross, they could have recoiled at the ghastly sight as others had.

We have no way of knowing how impacted they were by what they had witnessed and by what they had done. We also have no way of knowing how bewildered they were to soon learn that Jesus had risen from the dead **(Matthew**

28:6), that graves were opened, that many saints arose and appeared to many in the holy city **(Matthew 27:53)**, that He had appeared to and spoken to His eleven disciples three times. After all, they had both handled His body and they knew that body was dead. We cannot grasp their awe during the forty days when Jesus showed Himself alive following His passion by many infallible proofs. **(Acts 1:3)**

The following was written by Luke, the brother of Titus and only Gentile writer of the New Testament:
   Acts 1:3 (speaking of chosen apostles) To whom he showed himself alive after his passion by many infallible proofs, being seen by them forty days, and speaking of the things pertaining to the kingdom of God ...

And as Paul wrote in:
   Ephesians 2:10 For we are his workmanship created in Christ Jesus unto good works, which God hath before ordained that we should walk in them.

We have a choice. We can recoil, ignore, or carelessly botch the assignments He has chosen for us. Or we can cherish, embrace, and delight in them for His glory.

>   **Psalm 40:8** (written by King David)
>   I delight to do thy will, O my God ...

Embracing God's will is a sure way of delighting both God and yourself. Though our assignments do not equal the one given Joseph of Arimathaea and Nicodemus, they still can be difficult and not easily accomplished. During our lifetime, we cannot fully understand all the paths God has chosen that we walk to glorify Jesus. We can rest assured, just as God knew who to choose to minister to Jesus' body, He knows today who He can trust to do the same.

In a sense, the sometimes broken, bruised, bloodied body of Jesus (the church) is still being handled by saints assigned to its care; mainly pastors who must prayerfully and skillfully do so.

Included in Paul's farewell to the elders of the church at Ephesus was this:

Acts 20:28 Take heed, therefore, unto yourselves, and to all the flock, over which the Holy Spirit hath made you overseers, to feed the church of God, which he hath purchased with his own blood.

Paul wrote in **1st Corinthians 12:27**
"Now ye are the body of Christ ..."

THE NEXT WORST ASSIGNMENT

Proverbs 27:1 Boast not thyself of tomorrow; for thou knowest not what a day may bring forth.

Everyone would agree that we are many times clueless as to what will unfold from day-to-day in our own life. And, whereas we may not know what our future holds, we know who holds our future.

So it was for Simon and his sons, Alexander and Rufus, as they journeyed thirty-two days from Cyrene in the north central African country of Libya to Jerusalem to celebrate the Feast of Passover. It was a hazardous pilgrimage fraught with perils from bandits and beasts. (Much like our pilgrimage to the glory world).

Joseph of Arimathea and Nicodemus loved Jesus and knew He was the Son of God. They went to His cross to fulfill their assignments. But this unsuspecting man, Simon, may have been one of the most oblivious persons to have has ever lived.

Mark 15:21 And they compel one Simon, of Cyrene, who passed by, coming out of the country, the father of Alexander and Rufus, to bear his cross.

Only the Gospel of Mark, the last written of the three synoptic gospels, tells of his sons, Alexander and Rufus, being with him. **(Mark 15:21)** The Gospel of Luke adds that Simon had just come from the country. He would have been tired from travelling and wouldn't have expected being compelled (forced) to carry the patibulum of a condemned Jew who had said He was the Son of God. It was a repulsive demand; a demand he could not have ignored.

As an unsuspecting passer-by compelled to comply, Simon lightened our Savior's too heavy load; a load He could no longer carry alone. No doubt the precious Blood of Jesus touched this man who had only traveled to observe the Feast of Passover **(Mark 15:21)** but who would observe the perfect Passover Lamb of God being sacrificed for the sins of all mankind.

Jesus was crucified between two malefactors, (meaning, "people who did evil.") They were not both scourged and crucified as He was. Roman soldiers were extremely cruel but weren't known to both scourge and crucify a man. Though Jesus had forewarned His disciples that He would be both scourged and crucified, **(Matthew 20:19, Luke 18:33)** it was unconceivable to them.

Alexander and Rufus were not only old enough to make the strenuous journey to Jerusalem but they were also old enough to receive the message that the promised Messiah had been brutally mocked, scourged, and crucified. They knew, too, that their father had aided Him in sharing His load.

After Simon completed his assignment, we are not given more information concerning him. But surely, he was a special man chosen by God for an appalling task. His sons had seen their father bear Messiah's cross and had seen their father's bloodied clothes and hands. They had seen the soldiers bow before Jesus in mockery. And they had seen the thorn-crowned King impaled to the cross. Surely they heard Him pray, "Father, forgive them; they know not what they do."

Rufus, along with his mother, was honored by Paul in **Romans 16:13** which he wrote some twenty-four years after the death, burial, and resurrection of Jesus. Paul recognized Rufus, Simon of Cyrene's son, as chosen by the Lord and said his mother was as his own.

OUR LITTLE SECRET

Our local newspaper recently re-printed a report of Senator John Breaux recalling hitting a roadblock as a rookie member of the U.S. House of Representatives in 1972. For more than a year he had tried to win funding for a particular project in his district but to no avail. So he went to his Louisiana colleague, Senator Lindy Boggs. Senator Breaux said she then approached Speaker of the House Senator Tip O'Neill while the House was in session and whispered in his ear for a full two minutes. She returned and said, "John, it's done." Stunned by her confident casual remark, the amazed rookie senator asked, "What in the world did you tell him?" She answered, "I can't tell you, dear, that's our little secret."
This incident sounds like the old adage, "It's not what you know but who you know." And it contains spiritual truths reverberating throughout.

The rookie senator had become frustrated trying to work through the problem on his own. Sound familiar? He sought assistance from someone with clout. That person knew that the man with authority to grant the request was approachable; that he would heed a mere whisper.

Learning from experience, my friend, is not as painful as not learning from experience. After becoming a Christian, we learn early on that trying to resolve a problem on our own can become a disastrous disappointment. Yet, self-reliance is a commonly traveled path pitted with roadblocks for those not seeking guidance from the Lord.

Fortunately, the God-designed curriculum for His children is the blessing of ever-increasing intimacy with Him.

John 13:13-16 records the beginning of this intimacy. In these verses, Jesus taught the twelve disciples to be servants.

After Judas Iscariot departed, He welcomed the eleven as friends.
John 15:15 Henceforth I call you not servants; for the servant knoweth not what his lord doeth; but I have called you friends; for all things that I have heard of my Father I have made known unto you.

From servant to friend is quite a transition. You know friends tell their secrets to each other. And what a friend we have in Jesus who ever-liveth to make intersession. **(Hebrews 7:25)**

An even greater level of intimacy was made known by Jesus as He spoke to Mary Magdalene at the sepulcher after His death, burial, and resurrection.

John 20:17 Jesus saith unto her, Touch me not; for I am not yet ascended to my Father. But go to <u>my brethren</u>, and say unto them, I ascend unto my Father and your Father, and to my God and your God.

Jesus returned to His burial place to comfort the grieving Mary Magdalene even before ascending. His mission of reconciliation had been achieved. Notice how He emphasized "my Father, your Father, my God, your God, and my brethren." He didn't say, "go to my servants or go to my friends," but specifically said, "go to my brethren."

From servant to friend, and then to brethren

Romans 8:16-17 The Spirit himself beareth witness with our spirit, that we are the children of God; and if children, then heirs – heirs of God and joint heirs with Christ ...

Here are but a few benefits of the family of God, and they are <u>our little secret</u>.

Hebrews 4:16 Let us, therefore, come boldly unto the throne of grace, that we may obtain mercy, and find grace to help in time of need.

As brethren, we have unlimited access to the One who has all power. Jesus spoke these words to His eleven disciples following His resurrection:
Matthew 28:18 ... All power (authority) is given unto me in heaven and in earth.

You may be a rookie who has hit a roadblock. You may need to whisper a prayer to the ever-listening all-powerful Savior. You will discover that knowing Jesus is too wonderful for words. And remember, sometimes it's not what you know but who you know that really matters.

PA FORD PLOWED STRAIGHT
and
HE USED HIS CIPHERING PENCIL

Everybody who knew "Pa" Zeke Ford knew that he couldn't read his own name in boxcar letters. He was a sharecropper farmer known for feeding his family well. Pa Ford's good character and strong work ethic had earned him favor with the town's banker. Whatever amount of money was needed until his crop came in was extended based on his X signature alone.

> **Proverbs 22:1** A good name is rather to be chosen than great riches ...

Though poor, like most people in those parts, he saw to it that his wife, four sons, and two daughters were never without. It was also well-known that he kept a drunkard's wife and children fed too. His grown daughter took him to the big city of New Orleans to see the sights. She chuckled as she recalled him standing on a street corner and seeing the crowds of people and asking in childlike wonderment, "How does God feed all these people?"

One day, Daniel, his youngest son, asked, "Daddy how do you always plow your rows straight as an arrow?" His method was simple, "Son, do you see that fence post across over yonder? I keep my eye on it and I never look back."

Luke 9:59-61 tells of two men who wanted to follow Jesus but who wanted other things more and both responded with let "me first" do this and that. (By the way, neither were heard from again.)

Luke 9:62 And Jesus said unto him, no man, having put his hand to the plough (plow), and looking back, is fit for the kingdom of God.

And neither can we plow through the field of life while looking back. Keep your eyes on the goal of walking worthily. Scripture instructs us to "Set your affections on things above, not on the things of the earth."
(Colossians 3:2)

Hebrews 11:15 And truly, if they had been mindful of that country from which they came out, they might have had an opportunity to return.

Be aware that the enemy of your soul will leave a door of enticement open. This strategy does not ensnare those whose hearts are anchored in Jesus.

Pa Ford was a hardworking man who never gave up or gave in. When the entire farming community flooded causing crop failures, he told his sons they were going to plant cotton anyway. Other farmers felt this was ill-advised but Pa Ford persevered. His sons reported that year's cotton was four feet high and so sturdy that a child could climb its stalks. It made a bumper crop and allowed Pa to shower much-needed blessings on his family.

Proverbs 20:4 The sluggard will not plow by reason of the cold; therefore shall he beg in harvest and have nothing.

For years Pa Ford had driven his wife to church services and waited outside along with other reluctant husbands. That must have been a peculiar sight. It was a long time coming, but Pa Ford was finally persuaded to attend a service with his wife, Lettie. This was a special service ordained of God. Pa Ford's heart was changed in an instant as he responded to the preaching of the word of God. His destiny was then set after receiving the glorious baptism of the Holy Ghost. What joy flooded his soul! He radiated the joy of the Lord and immersed himself in the Lord's presence. An undeniable conversion had taken place. Pa Ford was a new man; a free man.

Unfortunately, his new-found peace evaporated when he cursed a mule. He naively believed this deed doomed his soul. (The devil doesn't mind what you trip on, just as long as you trip). Pa Ford wandered in misery thinking there was no way for him to be received back by God. Over a period of time, his wife and others convinced him otherwise. He did come back to the Lord and henceforth stuck like Velcro.

In **Luke 14:28** we learn of Jesus counseling would-be disciples to "count the cost."

Counting the cost was something that Pa Ford would do often. Though not educated, he was still a smart man. Seeing him busily jotting numbers on paper with his "ciphering pencil" was a fairly common sight. When asked, "Pa, whatcha doing?" he would say, "Oh, I'm ciphering." His two and a fourth-inch blue ciphering pencil with a nub of an eraser is today a treasured family relic of a man who ciphered before signing. A great deal of heartache can be avoided when we cipher before signing on a dotted line obligating ourselves to hundreds of "easy" monthly payments.

Pa Ford's legacy for his children and his children's children is to keep your eyes on the goal, don't look back, and cipher before signing. That's the wise council from a man who has "been there and done that."

THE CONVERSION OF PAUL

Who was this man, Paul, and why was he chosen by God as an apostle to the Gentiles? Saul, his circumcision name means, "asked for." After his conversion, he chose the Latin name, "Paul," which means, "little." He may have used a Roman name in voluntary humility and to more closely identify with Gentiles. Paul is mentioned 167 times between **Acts 13:9 and 2nd Peter 3:15.** The only other man named Saul in the Bible was King Saul.

Acts 23:6 tells us that he was a Pharisee and the son of a Pharisee. **Acts 22:3** states that he was a Jew who was born in the Roman Empire and was brought up "at the feet of Gamaliel." Gamaliel was the head or high priest of the Sanhedrin that controlled the internal government of Judea and consisted of seventy elders, plus the high priest. This civil council could not impose a sentence of death, which is why Jesus had to be tried before Pilate **(John 18:31-40)** after being tried by the Sanhedrin.

No more unlikely candidate for salvation could have been found than Paul. Regardless of what his life had been, God had determined that he would be a chosen vessel unto Him. We don't have to look far to see other unlikely candidates, or look in a mirror at another one. This Pharisee and son of a Pharisee had religious pride as the root of his aggressive persecution of Christians.

God knew that Paul needed a sudden and dramatic conversion, and it was no problem for Him to provide one.

One thing is sure; all true believers have had a personal conversion <u>experience</u> that they remember and cherish.

Daniel 4:37 tells of King Nebuchadnezzar speaking of God and saying, "…those that walk in pride he is able to abase."

And such was the case with Paul who considered his religious training to be a source of accomplishment. Perhaps God chose to deal with him in these areas because his religious pride would prevent him from truly serving him. If God does not choose to interrupt (or disrupt) our lives, we would continue on in a way that "seemeth right" unto us. Praise God for His intervention!

Psalm 18:25-26 With the merciful thou wilt show thyself merciful; with the upright thou wilt show thyself upright; with the pure thou wilt show thyself pure; and with the perverse thou wilt show thyself opposed.

God knows the hearts of all people. He knows how to deal appropriately with each one. Here's a sad commentary:
John 2:24-25 But Jesus did not commit himself unto them, because he knew all men, and needed not that any should testify of man; for he knew what was in man.

The following was written by Paul while imprisoned in Rome after his life's focus had been changed by God:
Philippians 3:3-14 For we are the circumcision, who worship God in the Spirit, and rejoice in Christ Jesus, and have no confidence in the flesh. Though I might also have confidence in the flesh. If any other man thinketh

that he hath reasons for which he might trust in the flesh, I more: Circumcised the eight day, of the stock of Israel, of the tribe of Benjamin, a Hebrew of the Hebrews; as touching the law, a Pharisee; concerning zeal, persecuting the church; touching the righteousness which is of the law, blameless. But what things <u>were gain</u> to me, those things I counted loss for Christ. Yea doubtless, and I count all things but loss, for the excellency of the knowledge of Christ Jesus, my Lord; for whom I suffer the loss of all things, and do count them but dung, that I may win Christ, and be found in him, not having mine own righteousness, which is of the law, but that which is through the faith of Christ, the righteousness which is of God by faith; <u>that I may know him</u>, and the power of his resurrection, and the fellowship of his suffering, being made conformable unto his death, if by any means I might attain unto the resurrection of the dead. Not as though I had already attained, either were already perfect; but I follow after, if that I may apprehend that for which also I am apprehended of Christ Jesus. Brethren, I count not myself to have apprehended; but this one thing I do, forgetting those things which are behind, and reaching forth unto those things which are before, I press toward the mark for the prize of the high calling of God in Christ Jesus.

Anyone who reads this writing of Paul will surely recognize his love of God and devotion to the truth.

Paul wrote the following to Timothy recorded in:
    1st Timothy 1:12-13 And I thank Christ Jesus, our Lord, who hath enabled me, in that he counted me

faithful, putting me into the ministry, who was a blasphemer, and a persecutor, and injurious; but I obtained mercy, because I did it ignorantly in unbelief.

Numbers 15:28-31 states that the priest was to make atonement for the soul who sins through ignorance.

We know that Jesus is our High Priest who ever liveth to make intercession on our behalf and that His Blood provided the perfect and acceptable sacrifice.
(Hebrews 7:25)

Chapter 9 of the Book of Acts details Paul's conversion. And, by conversion, we mean what occurs when men are influenced by divine grace upon their souls, and their whole lives are changed. The Book of Acts is full of these rich conversion stories. **Acts 16:** tells of the Philippian jailer, **Acts 8:** of the Ethiopian eunuch, **Acts 10:** of Cornelius and his household, and **Acts 16:** tells of Lydia. However, **Chapter 9:** is not the only time Paul's conversion is recorded. He told the story two other times **(Acts 22** and **26)**.

Acts 9:1-3 And Saul, yet breathing out threatenings and slaughter against the disciples of the Lord, went unto the high priest, and desired of him letters to Damascus to the synagogues, that if he found any of this way, whether they were men or women, he might bring them bound unto Jerusalem. And, as he journeyed, he came near Damascus, and suddenly there shone round about him a light from heaven.

Notice the strong words used to describe Paul's activities, "breathing out threatenings and slaughter." No one can be more dangerous than a religious zealot who believes he's on a mission from God. As a religious zealot, Paul showed no mercy on those who called upon the name of Jesus and yet, God had determined that Paul be a recipient of unmerited favor and grace, just as we are.

Damascus, the capital of Syria today, is one of the world's oldest cities. As Saul (Paul) journeyed on the road to Damascus with the full intent of destroying the work of God, the hand of the Lord <u>suddenly</u> moved to re-direct his life. When God chooses to reveal Himself, many times He moves suddenly and in unexpected ways which catapults a person into making sudden and unexpected changes.

Acts 9:4-5 And he fell to the earth, and heard a voice saying unto him, 'Saul, Saul, why persecutest thou me?' And he said, 'Who art thou, Lord?' And the Lord said, 'I am Jesus, whom thou persecutest; it is hard for thee to kick against the pricks (goads).

Identifying with His Church (His Bride), Jesus twice made it clear who Saul was persecuting. He called Saul's name twice just as He had earlier when He rebuked Martha and later Simon Peter. Notice that this religious Pharisee, who was brought up at the feet of Gamaliel had to ask, "Who art thou Lord?" No amount of religious training will teach us to recognize the voice of God. We must learn this on our own. It is not good for anyone to "kick against the pricks (goads)" which is to "offer unavailing resistance to superior power."

Acts 9:6 And he, trembling and astonished, said, 'Lord, what wilt thou have me to do?' and the Lord said unto him, 'Arise, and go into the city, and it shall be told thee what thou must do.

So now the man who had been "breathing out threatenings and slaughter" is lying on the ground "trembling and astonished" and asking, "What wilt thou have me to do?" Paul's life had been interrupted, disrupted so that the great eternal purposes of God might be accomplished through him. (Has this happened to you also?)

In the sixth verse, Paul began to be directed by God in a step-by-step process that was only revealed as he obeyed. This is how God deals with His own. We are never given the complete "game plan." He requires that we walk by faith and not by sight or in our own understanding.

Paul wasn't told that he would be used to write most of the New Testament and that it would be used by God to convert countless millions of souls for over two thousand years. And he wasn't told that he would experience imprisonments, be beaten five times with forty stripes (save one), three times beaten with rods, stoned, shipwrecked (and the list goes one in **2nd Corinthians 11:23-28**). At this point, all he is told is all he needs to know. His obedience determined his future usefulness to the Lord, and ours does too.

Acts 9:7 And the men who journeyed with him stood speechless, hearing a voice, but seeing no man.

When this story is re-told in Acts 22, it states that the men with him saw the light but heard not the voice that spoke to Paul. It is thought that they could not understand what the voice was saying. And so it is with us. How can others understand what God is speaking to us as individuals, and how can we cannot fully comprehend what the Lord is speaking to someone else?

Acts 9:8-9 And Saul arose from the earth, and when his eyes were opened, he saw no man; but they led him by the hand, and brought him unto Damascus. And he was three days without sight, neither did eat nor drink.

So the high and mighty Paul is now-blinded and has to be led by others. He had thought he controlled the destiny of others only to find that he didn't even control his own. We were told at the beginning that God moved "suddenly;" however, now we find that he required Paul to go three days without further instruction, and he does so without sight, food, or drink. Instead of commanding the destruction of others, now he waits to hear from the God of his fathers what his own future would be. Can you imagine what was going on in this Pharisee's mind during those three days? Interesting.

Acts 9:10 And there was a certain disciple at Damascus, named Ananias; and to him said the Lord in a vision, 'Ananias', and he said, 'Behold, I *am here*, Lord.

Notice that, when the Lord spoke to him in a vision, Ananias recognized it was the Lord immediately, unlike the religious Pharisee Saul.

The Bible mentions three men named Ananias, and all three are in the Book of Acts; Ananias, the disciple at Damascus, Ananias, the husband of Sapphira, and Ananias, the high priest.

Acts 9:11-12 And the Lord said unto him, Arise, and go into the street which is called Straight, and inquire in the house of Judas for one called Saul of Tarsus; <u>for behold he prayeth</u>, and hath seen in a vision a man, named Ananias, coming in and putting his hand on him, that he might receive his sight.

"...<u>For behold he prayeth</u>." Wouldn't you love to have heard his three days of praying while blinded? God directed Ananias onto the street that is called Straight. Paul is now on the straight and narrow way, and God will ensure that he stays on it. God knows exactly what street you are on, too.

The Book of Acts records "the acts" of the apostles of the Lord Jesus Christ as they began to minister with power and authority as Jesus had done. Ananias was told to lay his hands on Paul, as Jesus would have done, that he might receive his sight. Obviously, the same God who struck him down could restore his sight as well. However, God now chooses to do many of His works through men.

Acts 9:13-14 Then Ananias answered, 'Lord, I have heard by many of this man, how much evil he hath done to thy saints at Jerusalem; and here (at Damascus) he hath authority from the chief priests to bind all that call on thy name.

Ananias had a genuine concern that "this man hath done much evil" and had a well-known reputation among the saints. Precious Ananias explained his concerns to the all-knowing (omniscient) God.

Acts 9:15-16 But the Lord said unto him, 'Go thy way; for he is a chosen vessel unto me, to bear my name before the Gentiles, and kings, and the children of Israel; for I will show him how great things he must suffer for my name's sake.

God comforted Ananias in assuring him that, although Paul had done much evil, he now would be used as a vessel of honor. And now, instead of causing suffering, he would be called to suffer. Hmmm. Neither Paul nor Ananias could have imagined that God would use Paul to write thirteen epistles comprising slightly over 30% of the New Testament.

Acts 9:17 Ananias went his way, and entered into the house; and putting his hands on him, said, '<u>Brother Saul</u>, the Lord, even <u>Jesus</u>, that appeared unto thee in the way as thou camest, hath sent me, that thou mightest receive thy sight, and be filled with the Holy Ghost.

Just as God had instructed him to "Go thy way," we find here in verse 17 that he "went his way." And he went with peace in his heart knowing that he was obeying God. What an incalculable value it is to know His voice. Ananias went, as he was directed, and completed his assigned task. He is not mentioned again in scripture. He didn't embark on a worldwide televangelist crusade as the "man God used to pray for Paul." ☺ With his mission complete, he merely returned to his everyday life without accolades.

I have not found another instance where someone was given the title of "Brother." Many are called "a brother" but are not addressed as "Brother" as a proper name. Surely, Ananias did this to assure Paul that he accepted him as a fellow believer. Ananias chose to identify preciously what "Lord" he was speaking of by saying, "the Lord, <u>even Jesus</u>." It was time for Paul to acknowledge Jesus as Lord himself.

Ananias spoke in a straightforward manner only the words God had given him, "Receive thy sight and be filled with the Holy Ghost," and the results were immediate. The prophet Jonah spoke only the eight words God had given him for the City of Nineveh, and the results were immediate, too. It has been said, "Some are sent and some just went." God is able to accomplish His purpose through those who are sent by Him, and that is what He did with Ananias and Jonah. And will through you, too!

Acts 9:18-19 And immediately there fell from his eyes as it had been scales; and he received sight, and arose, and was baptized. And when he had received food, he was strengthened. Then was Saul certain days with the disciples who were at Damascus.

Wouldn't you think it would be impossible to see with scales on your eyes? Pity the person whom the god of this world has blinded and especially those who have been blinded by religion. But, as with Paul, God is able to remove those scales at the appropriate moment.

Now that God had sovereignly changed the course of his life, Paul had fellowship with the saints at Damascus instead of destroying them. Just as Paul sought the fellowship of those who had experienced the Lord, we also seek fellowship (fellows-in-the-same-ship). There is nothing like the camaraderie shared by the saints of God.

Acts 9:20-22 And immediately he preached Christ in the synagogues, that he was the Son of God. But all that heard him were amazed, and said, 'Is not this he that destroyed them who called on this name in Jerusalem, and came here for that intent, that he might bring them bound unto the chief priests? But Saul increased the more in strength, and confounded the Jews who dwelt at Damascus, proving that this is the Christ.

Truly, the mercy of God experienced by Paul is well beyond what we can understand. Also, the number of souls saved through his converted life and ministry are more than we could number. Even before his martyrdom, Paul's writings were acknowledged to be scripture.

2nd Peter 3:16 As also in all his epistles, speaking in them of these things, in which are some things hard to be understood, which they that are unlearned and unstable wrest, <u>as they do also the other scriptures</u>, unto their own destruction.

Only God knows what He has purposed for each life, including yours.

PLAN WITH PRAYER
SAVE WITH PRUDENCE
SPEND WITH CONFIDENCE

God's understanding is infinite. His word tells us that He knows the number of hairs on our head, He knows the thoughts and intents of our heart, and He has made abundant provision for all needs.

Our Creator-ordained testing (or proving) reveals our true character. This is a good thing because, if we receive His reproof, we also will receive His praise:

1st Corinthians 4:5 ... the Lord ... will make manifest the counsels of the hearts; and then shall every man have praise of God.

The way we handle money can be a primary source of testing. Consider what Jesus said:

Luke 16:11 If, therefore, ye have not been faithful in the unrighteous mammon (money), who will commit to your trust the true riches?

I entered into a long-term process of learning about the use of money after having been propelled into the suddenly-single arena. When my daughter became a high school senior, there were months when the money ran out before the month did. I loved God and trusted Him to make a way. An unexpected phone call informed me that my income had been lopped off $500 a month. Since I knew Jesus to be my source, I prayed while walking through the house, "Lord, what are we going to do?" The Comforter's immediate response calmed my concern, "You'll have more with less." He merely told me all I needed to know. I never gave it another thought. I don't know how He did it, but I did have more with less.

He taught what I needed to know as I continued coursing through life trusting Him. Here's a tremendous gem shared by God:

> Plan With Prayer
>
> Save With Prudence
>
> Spend With Confidence

Have you ever noticed how God's solutions – His "formulas for success" are not complicated? Whereas, man's reasoning can be loaded with grandiose schemes that can actually worsen the outcome.

I still have a monthly income and expense record I began in 1990. At the beginning of each month's ledger I wrote what God had counseled, "Plan with Prayer, Save with Prudence, Spend with Confidence." God's tithe and offering were always the first entry. By some standards, my income would have been considered low (very low), however, I never had a financial need arise that I wasn't prepared to meet. I never had a debt, never paid a finance charge, or any late fee. I obeyed God's direction, until ...

After God blessed my life with a precious Christian husband, I got a little too happy – a little too confident. I leaped over the "Plan with Prayer, Save with Prudence" portion and dove into the "Spend with Confidence." Now mind you, I wasn't like an out-of-control tour bus careening down a mountain side. It's just that I wasn't doing the first two directives; Plan with Prayer, Save with Prudence. It was an expensive misadventure that I regret to this day.

Let's take a glimpse into the words of the prophet Haggai. The prophet's brief two chapter message contains four terse "wake up calls" from God who had had enough. The temple foundation had been laid some sixteen to twenty years prior and yet no other work had been done.

The following quote from Haggai is not something I want to present "out of context" so to speak, but I want to use it to emphasize what happened to me in not obeying the Lord.

Haggai 1:6-7 Ye have sown much, and bring in little; ye eat, but have not enough; ye clothe yourselves, but there is none warm; and he that earneth wages earneth wages to put in a bag with holes. Thus saith the Lord of hosts: Consider your ways.

By circumventing God's direction, I had put our wages into a bag with holes. The outcome wasn't pleasant. The Lord's chastening, though appreciated, wasn't pleasant either. This is written to encourage you to <u>consider your ways</u> and that you endeavor to make God's ways your ways.

PRAYER SECRETS REVEALED

Brother Martin answered the knock on his door with no thought of who or what might be on the other side. Standing there were two young men who introduced themselves as Christians who wanted to share their faith with him. Brother Martin, a pastor himself, cordially welcomed them into his home while thinking he would delight in sharing his faith with them and learning of theirs. (Wrong ☹)

Seated on his couch between the two, he listened patiently. He knew their beliefs were more than a little left of center. But when they leaned forward looking at him and whispered their deep prayer secret, it was all Brother Martin could do to maintain his composure.

THEIR SECRET: God doesn't hear any prayer that's not spoken in the original King James language.

It would appear these Bible scholars didn't know that Jesus, while suffering on the cross, spoke and prayed in Aramaic.

In another occurrence, the following real illustration, is a prime example of faith-gone-wrong.

Jane took refuge in a mental evaluation clinic for a "time out" period away from her highly dysfunctional family. The doors of pandemonium had swung open at Jane's house; it was time for her to take a rest alone with God. Jane, herself a nurse, knew this could be a beneficial time; a time of recuperating and rebounding. When interviewed by the admitting nurse, she emphasized that she was a Christian and that she knew God would heal her. With a wave of her hand and a joyful smile, the nurse dismissed her trust in God, "Oh, it doesn't matter what you believe. See that light bulb? There was a patient here who believed that light bulb was going to heal her."

HER SECRET: It doesn't matter what you believe.

Jane knew God and knew He would deliver her from mental anguish and confusion and He did. Jane's family underwent a healthy restoration, and God received all of the glory!

In this last sad example, Marsha, a very well-educated woman, pressed a hand-written prayer onto my palm, and said, "Pray this for seven-days and your prayer will be answered." I don't know what had influenced her to share this prayer secret. I read the first sentence of the suggested prayer and was too baffled to answer. She walked away without offense. She never asked if her prayer suggestion was followed.

The prayer began, "Kiss baby Jesus upon your knee ..." I never got past that beginning request. I was aghast that this well-educated woman believed Jesus was caught in some sort of time warp. Not knowing what to say, I said nothing.

HER SECERT: Kiss baby Jesus upon your knee.

OUR SECRET

God's word tells us plainly who Jesus is:

1st Timothy 2:5 For there is one God; and one mediator between God and men, the man, Christ Jesus.

God's word says what He wants us to know.

Jeremiah 31:14 is quoted in: **Hebrews 8:10,11** ... I will put my laws into their mind, and write them in their hearts; and I will be to them a God, and they shall be to me a people.

Christians pray to the only God, who has made Himself known to them. He doesn't require a specific language, He is not a light bulb, and He is not dangling somewhere between infancy and manhood.

Paul wrote the epistle to the Romans during his third visit to Corinth. In it he encapsulated the desire of believers throughout the world:

Romans 10:1-2 Brethren, my heart's desire and prayer to God for Israel is, that they might be saved. For I bear them witness, that they have a zeal for God, but not according to knowledge.

I sometimes pray this and substitute my own family members' names for "Israel."

Zeal without knowledge is dangerous territory and provides the zealot with false security. Submit your every thought and belief to His scrutiny.

2nd Corinthians 13:5 Examine yourselves, whether you are in the faith; prove yourselves.

This examining of ourselves involves a deliberate effort to be transparent and to welcome His instruction and reproof. Being teachable is a key to our spiritual growth. People may say, "There is <u>no</u> God." Whereas, God's word says we are to all "<u>know</u> God." Some may say, "When people are praying, they are speaking to God." However, when the person praying hears God speaking, some may say they are crazy. The truth is that when believers begin to hear the voice of God, they know it's supernatural. It's absolutely super and it's natural!

TESTMONIES FROM LONG AGO

Leviticus 26:45 But I will for their sakes remember the covenant of their ancestors, whom I brought forth out of the land of Egypt in the sight of the heathen that I might be their God: I am the Lord.

Deuteronomy 7:9 ... the Lord thy God, he is God, the faithful God, who keepeth covenant and mercy with them who love him and keep his commandments unto a thousand generations ...

God honors the covenant made with our ancestors and we should too. One way for us to do that is to treasure and preserve their testimonies. The following five testimonies were preserved and published for God's glory and for your encouragement. I asked the Lord to let these saints know that their testimonies are being shared still.

Charlotte Cobb Powers   John Booker Powers

Vera Lee Lewis   Julia White Nichols

Elder A. W. Sassman

You, too, will leave a testimony, but remember that without a test, there is no testimony. Our "testing" proves who we are. The testing of some will only prove they were "testaphonies."

CHARLOTTE COBB POWERS

B: 11-03-1809 D: 07-15-1878

Sister Charlotte Cobb Powers, whose life was one of devotion to the good of others and whose end was perfect peace, resting in the atoning blood of Jesus, passed away like the setting of the sun. Calm, peaceful, and trusting, she passed down into the cool waters of death with the name of Jesus on her lips with no cloud intervening to obscure the smiles of an approving Father.

Sister Powers was one of those characters whose sweet, amiable disposition won at once the love and respect of all who knew her. Her hand was always ready to assist the needy.

Liberal to the calls of the church of her choice and supporting its institutions, she provided for the weary care-worn indigent. It was always her delight to welcome them to her home. Many who read these lines will call up many pleasant reminiscences of the past while enjoying the good things provided for their comfort by the skillful hands of Aunt Lottie.

Sister Powers was married twice. Her maiden name was Cobb. Her first marriage occurred in about 1836 to Abraham Billings with whom she lived until his death which occurred in about 1843.

In 1856, she was married again to John Booker Powers, with whom she lived until his death which occurred in about 1873.

By these marriages, she had no children, but she had the care of eight orphans, whom she raised to womanhood and manhood. Besides these, she had the care of four step-children.

Sister Powers was baptized in infancy by Rev. Lorenzo Dow and united with the Methodist Church when about thirty-five years of age and ever lived in the enjoyment of that sweet peace which comes from a hope well founded in Jesus.

Her life was unspotted and her death triumphant.

BY: RUFFIN T. DAVIS, PASTOR

JOHN BOOKER POWERS
B: 01-20-1806   D: 04-11-1873

John Booker Powers was born in East Feliciana Parish, Louisiana on January 20, 1806 and died, at his residence in East Baton Rouge Parish, on April 11, 1873, after suffering for a period of nine weeks.

Brother Powers professed religion and joined the Methodist-Episcopal Church in the year 1829 and was a member of the Methodist-Episcopal Church South at the time of his death.

I visited him in a short time after he was taken sick and found him glad to see me. While we read the Bible, sang hymns, and prayed he became happy and rejoiced in God. From this time he continued in the same frame of mind, always expressing himself as willing and ready to be absent from the body and present with the Lord. His physician told me that he had never seen anyone in a sane state of mind do desirous to die.

He was liberal with the means with which Heaven had blessed him, both to the Church and to the indigent.

During the war, the soldiers of the Northern Army burned the church-house where he held his membership. He saw it while it was yet burning and promised himself that, if he lived and had the means, when the war closed, he would rebuild the Church. He had the money and, at an expense of $500 or $600 to himself, built Bethel Church, the house we now worship in.

His house was a home for the Preachers. Thus lived and died one of the servants of God, and, when he came to leave the terrestrial body, he was prepared to leave a good testimony to his surviving friends.

May his wife, children, and friends be as well prepared to go when they are called hence.

N. B. Young

NOTE: John Booker Powers is buried in the Powers Cemetery on Gilead Road near Bluff Creek, Louisiana alongside his first wife, Elizabeth Browning, and some of their children.

The church he built was located at Indian Mound just off of Hwy 37 in East Baton Rouge Parish, Louisiana where Bethel Church is now located. His brother, James Powers, and his wife, Unity Blount Powers are buried in its cemetery.

VERA LEE'S DEATHBED CONFESSION

The following deathbed confession was written by Nona Freeman in, "Beloved Wide Spot."

Three months after the revival closed at Cypress, a distressed Guthrie Lewis came one morning with a request. "Sister Freeman, my wife, Vera Lee, is critically ill and unable to come to you. She wants to see you; will you come?"

"Certainly," I replied, "but she seemed fine during the revival meeting. What happened?" "The doctor says she has galloping leukemia and will only live a few more weeks at the most." He sighed deeply, "We'll expect you this afternoon."

Nothing Guthrie said prepared me for the pale shadow of a once beautiful young lady I found on the bed. Her white, almost-translucent hands fluttered as she indicated her weakness and asked for patient listening.

"You will travel far, Sister Freeman," she whispered, "and preach to multitudes of people. I'm compelled to give you a sermon illustration from the lips of a foolish one, and I hope you will use it over and over. Put your ear close to my lips so you can hear what I say."

I bent over to hear the tragic story told in utter weakness, with many pauses to rest. "A casual observer would have thought me a real Christian. I went through the motions knowing the right things to do and say, but my heart was not in it. I carefully did all the pastor expected, but while my lips voiced meaningless praise words, my mind toyed with every conceivable fantasy. Real worship is a concert from the heart, soul, and mind. I went through the actions of singing, testifying, praying, and listening to messages while in my head I cut out a new dress, planted flowers, painted the kitchen, visited friends and relations, or went shopping with limitless funds.

"Oh, my friend," tears trickled down the waxen cheeks, "if only I could go back one more time and sing one of those lovely old songs about the blood of Jesus – I would picture the cross and praise Him with deep gratitude for the precious low that redeemed me. When the leader said, 'let everyone pray' how fervently I would life my voice to the King. When the preacher opened the word, I would follow him in my Bible, make notes, and allow the living Truth to nourish my soul. I would have real concern and compassion for a lost world – and do something about it if I could. But – the dear Lord has assured me He'll take me to His house, but I will go with empty hands." I wept with her.

Her last words haunt me still:

"Whenever you think of me, warn others to be real, to serve God from the heart, and not to waste the precious fleeting moments."

I have tried.

JULIA WHITE NICHOLS

A Testimony

These comments were derived from:
LaSalle Parish History
Families Past and Present, page 53

W. T. "Babe" Nichols met and married Julia Asilea White, an orphan and devout Christian, in Lufkin, Texas. Everywhere they went, Momma started Sunday schools. About four years after they married, Momma was pregnant, and their two little children died of the summer sickness. Momma's brother, Locket, was knifed and died in her arms. Momma was very courageous. Her parents, three brothers, and three babies are buried in Lufkin, Texas. Yet, she had faith in the Lord. While Momma and Poppa were visiting his parents in Texarkana, Texas, another baby died and is buried there.

A plague came through the country and killed all the cattle and oxen. Poppa converted to mules for the wagons. Poppa led the wagons to Geneva, Texas, and a cyclone hit down. Momma prayed for their safety, and when she had a daughter years later she named her Geneva. Altogether, Momma had sixteen babies with seven living to womanhood and manhood.

After World War 1 ended, Poppa moved to Aimwell, Louisiana. They had two houses on their place, and Poppa tore the partition out of one, sent for a preacher, and made it a church.

When Momma started her last Sunday school, she became very ill, and a premature baby girl was born. As Momma lay dying, she asked that her children be brought to her side. She told them that she was going away, and if they lived the way she had taught them, they would come to where she was someday. She prayed for each child and asked the Lord to be with them when things were too hard for them. She then called her son-in-law to her side and said she wanted to give him something before she went away. Her words were, "Big boy, if you help sister with it (meaning the church and the Sunday school), you will love it. If you don't, it'll be a great burden to you." Being emotional, Fletcher went out to the woodpile. He looked and saw two filmy figures hover over the house. Two came down and three went away. He knew before they called him that Momma was gone.

Julia White Nichols had many heartaches and trials. She experienced many unexplained events, and she had victory in the Lord.

And speaking of those who have received the gift of life from God, the Bible has this to say:

Ecclesiastes 5:20 For he shall not much remember the days of his life, because God answereth him in the joy of his heart.

The Year Was 1939

The year was 1939 when Elder A. W. Sassman came to Catahoula Parish, Louisiana preaching repentance in Jesus name. He held a big revival on Fort Hill with the help of three area churches where he had held revivals. At the close of the revival at Harrisonburg, he received word from an area business to come to Jonesville, Louisiana. The following is taken from his book, "Signs, Wonders, and Miracles: The Story of My Life," (pages 42, 43).

In Harrisonburg, Louisiana there was a general mercantile store owned by the Brown brothers. They had one in Jonesville, also. The Brown brothers sent me word to come to Jonesville to get some of those hypocrites saved over there.

After this revival God spoke to me, "Son, I hold you responsible for fifty souls in Jonesville, Louisiana." Never had there been a Pentecostal meeting there. We pitched our tent and God blessed.

There was bad weather and the tent was getting old. I had a young preacher helping me. He'd stay around the tent, and every day we had to patch it up. The young preacher finally threw up his hands and said, "Oh, Lord, never bless me with a tent!" It was just work and worry. Finally, the tent tore up, and we finished up in the open air.

In three weeks' time, over forty received the Holy Ghost. The Lord spoke to my heart, "Now, son, I've got a man I want you to turn this work over to, and I want you to move on." The Lord wouldn't let me settle down enough to build a church. My evangelistic burden was so strong. The Lord said, "Over in the country, there's a fellow named Leonard Lofton. He's the man for the job."

The next day I drove to his house and knocked on the door. His wife answered, and I asked for Leonard, but I could hear him groaning and praying in the woods. I walked up to him and said, "Say, brother, what are you crying about?" He said, "This morning I got up and the Lord let me know He has a town where he wants me to go, and I'm trying to find out where it is." I said, "You quit praying. You come to Jonesville tonight. I've got a revival going, souls are being filled with the Holy Ghost, and now I'm going to turn my loudspeakers and pews over to you. I'm going to introduce you as the new pastor to go on with the work, and I'll preach my farewell service."

And, sure enough, he came. I preached my farewell service and introduced Brother Lofton as the pastor. He built a church there, and it's still there today.

THE ENOCH TESTIMONY

Let's focus on the following scriptures:

Genesis 5:24 And Enoch walked with God, and he was not; for God took him.

Hebrews 11:5 By faith Enoch was translated that he should not see death, and was not found, because God had translated him; for before his translation he had this testimony, that he pleased God.

Translated is a Greek word (#3346), meaning "transport, change sides." The term "rapture" is derived from the Latin word "raptus," which means "caught up, or caught away." It doesn't appear in scripture.

However, the following does:

1st Thessalonians 4:17 Then we which are alive and remain shall be <u>caught up</u> together with them in the clouds, to meet the Lord in the air; and so shall we ever be with the Lord.

Speaking of saints who enter the heavenly kingdom:

Revelation 12:11 And they overcame him (Satan) by the Blood of the Lamb, and by the word of their testimony; and they loved not their lives unto the death.

Always keep in mind, if you intend to make the rapture, you must have "The Enoch Testimony." Walk with God and be pleasing unto Him as you overcome the adversary through the merits of His atoning Blood.

The grief-stricken Job lamented:

Job 1:21 And said, Naked came I out of my mother's womb, and naked shall I return there.

And Paul wrote to Timothy:

1st Timothy 6:7 For we brought nothing into this world, and it is certain we can carry nothing out.

However, just like you and I will do, Job and Paul each carried something out with them – their testimony!

Make it your goal to be pleasing unto God, and you won't be ashamed on Judgment Day.

THEORY VERSES EXPERIENCE

It has been said that the person with the experience is never at the mercy of the person with the theory. Let's consider the following allegory with respect to "Theory verses Experience." Suppose you were told that the old electrical wall socket was dead that the power that once flowed from it had somehow disappeared. No one knows what happened to the power or if it will ever return.

Now let's further suppose that you are in a large room filled with books containing the theories of scholars regarding what we will name the "Electrical Power Disappearance Theory." The scholars' thoughts are deep and well-intended. Their conclusions are based on the latest research. But they are lacking one thing: EXPERIENCE. However, if you were to put one finger into the old wall socket, you would experience for yourself that it is full of power. You might even jump, shout, and tell others that you experienced its great power. From that moment on, whatever written or said disputing its existence is of no concern.

Thank God for the empowering of the Holy Ghost which enables us to be overcomers by experiencing the true power of God.

Fern Jones (1923-1996), a popular gospel songwriter and singer, wrote, "I Was There When It Happened, So I Guess I Ought To Know." The lyrics speak of commonly shared experiences of those who have received Jesus into their hearts.

The lyrics include words like:
I know the very moment He saved me, I have never doubted, I know when He forgave me, He took away my heavy burdens, He gave me peace within.

My friend, how can you go wrong with experiencing such things like that? Believers relish re-living experiences in the Lord over and over. They are the rejoicing of our hearts. I wouldn't trade anything in this world for what He has done for me. And, to think, He didn't have to do it.

In Psalm 34 and 38, King David expressed jubilation over victories in the Lord. Believers appreciate his words because they have experienced the same.

Psalm 34:3 Oh, magnify the Lord with me, and let us exalt his name together.

Those who have experienced the goodness and mercy of the Lord are eager to join with others in exalting Him.

Psalm 34:8 Oh, taste and see that the Lord is good; blessed is the man who trusteth in him.

The simple statement is an invitation to "taste and see" or experience for yourself; once you have done that you won't be satisfied with less.

Oh, what a marvelous life and a thrilling eternity.

THERE REMAINETH, THEREFORE A REST ...

Hebrews 4:9 There remaineth, therefore, a rest to the people of God.

Only when we drop the robe of flesh and enter His eternal Sabbath will we have complete rest. But during our lifetimes, He intends for His people to have rest as they abide in faith in Him.

Learning to abide in Him can be a long process spotted with much frustration. Woven into your journey's mosaic will be seasons of waiting while God remains silent, (CLUE: A teacher remains silent during a test). If you do not enjoy your time of waiting before Him, you will not enjoy most of your life, since most of our lives are lived while waiting before Him.

As our Creator, He paces us at a pace that's right for us. A hurdle jumper is a well-trained disciplined athlete. He anticipates each hurdle and gracefully overcomes by being alert and prepared. He goes at a pace that's right for him expecting to overcome obstacles on his path. As followers of Christ, we learn to do the same.

Notice God's sorrow expressed in:
    Isaiah 30:15 For thus saith the Lord, The Holy One of Israel: In returning and rest ye shall be saved; In quietness and in confidence shall be your strength: <u>And ye would not</u>.

The verses following outlines an already-in-place action plan, which excluded God.

Isaiah 30:15-16 For this saith the Lord God, the Holy One of Israel: In returning and rest shall ye be saved; in quietness and in confidence shall be your strength: and ye would not. But ye said, No; for we will flee upon horses. Therefore shall ye flee. And, We will ride upon the swift. Therefore, shall those who pursue you be swift.

Some scriptures referring to a horse can be a cloaked allusion to depending on the strength of the flesh. Isaiah may have used this as an aphorism for them trusting in their own selves for deliverance.

In the verses following Isaiah 30:16, God revealed His decision to wait before becoming gracious to them again. Talk about a self-imposed limitation! Since they chose not to return to Him and His rest, they would not have quietness, confidence, or strength.

Isaiah 11:10 And in that day there shall be a root of Jesse, who shall stand for an ensign (flag) of the peoples; <u>to him shall the Gentiles seek, and his rest shall be glorious</u>.

Who is this root of Jesse? Root is Greek word (#4491), meaning, "descendant or branch of family stock."

>Salmon begot Boaz of Rahab
>Boaz begot Obed of Ruth
>Obed begot Jesse
>Jesse begot David, the king

Kind David was descended from the tribe of Judah, as were both Mary and Joseph.

Revelation 22:16 ... (Jesus) I am the root and the offspring of David, the bright and morning star.

Matthew 11:28 (Jesus) Come unto me, all ye that labor and are <u>heavy laden</u>, and I will give you rest. Take my yoke upon you, and learn of me; for I am meek and lowly in heart, and ye shall find rest for your souls. For my yoke is easy and my burden light.

Yes, in the earthly realm, His rest is glorious. We have yet to bask in His eternal rest. Oh, but we will!

The word "laden" is noteworthy. The following two scriptures link "laden" with sin:
2nd Timothy 3:6 For of this sort are they who creep into houses, and lead captive silly women who are <u>laden</u> with sins, led away with various lusts ...
Isaiah 1:4 Ah, sinful nation, a people <u>laden</u> with iniquity, a seed of evildoers, children that are corrupters ...

Those who are truly resting in Him are not laden with sin. They are focused on the Lord and what pleases Him.

Media sources are filled with evil that allures through the lust of the flesh. The prince of the power of the air (waves), infiltrates minds that are not focused on God.

Mark recorded some helpful truth given by Jesus and chances are you may never have heard it preached:

Mark 6:30-31 And the apostles gathered themselves together unto Jesus, and told him all things, both what they had taught. And he said unto them, Come aside (apart) into a desert place, and rest a while; for there were many coming and going, and <u>they had no leisure</u> so much as to eat.

Resting in God is not complacency. Taking your leisure is what Jesus taught. Saints resting in Him don't have time to be overcharged with the cares of this world.

REVEREND IKE

The Not So Reverend Frederick J. Eikerenkoetter, II

B: 6-1-1935   D: 7-30-2009

The Reverend Ike (as he was known) lived a total 27,088 days. The son of African-American parents – his father a Baptist minister and his mother a teacher. The Rev. Ike was born in Ridgeland, South Carolina. At age fourteen, he felt the call to preach and became an associate pastor of a local Pentecostal church.

The path Reverend Ike choose took him as far from his home as it did from God. At the time of his death, his prosperity-based "ministry" was receiving a million dollars in monthly donations, owned sixteen Rolls-Royces, a number of Bentleys and other vehicles in addition to six palatial residences. His "ministry" was then based in New York City where his prosperity theology flourished. His adherents flocked to and filled Madison Square Garden to hear his unabashed love of money sermons.

Reverend Ike's messages were broadcast on ten major television networks and his radio sermons were heard daily on 1,700 stations. I well remember unsuspectingly tuning in to one of his radio broadcasts. His booming words were, "The lack of money is the root of all evil. (A favorite declaration of his). Don't leave your money to your heathen children to squander. Leave it to my ministry, and you'll prosper." I felt shocked and saddened at the same time.

The not-so-reverend Reverend Ike said the Bible was the greatest book on Mind Science and that he was frustrated trying to please some kind of a tyrannical God in the sky. Following his death, his son, Xavier, took the reins of his father's earthly kingdom.

Peter, speaking of false prophets and false teacher, wrote:
2nd Peter 2:3 And through covetousness shall they, with feigned words, make merchandise of you; ...

Words of wisdom and warning from God's word:

Proverbs 30:8-9 Remove far from me vanity and lies; give me neither poverty nor riches; feed me with food convenient for me, lest I be full, and deny thee, and say, Who is the Lord? Or lest I be poor, and steal, and take the name of my God in vain.

1st Timothy 6:7 For we brought nothing into this world, and it is certain we can bring nothing out.

However, as was mentioned previously, everyone brings their testimony. May we each endeavor to walk worthily of the high calling in Christ Jesus.

THEY ALL TOLD THE TRUTH

After leaving Mt. Sinai, Moses and the people of God traveled three days to Kadesh-barnea. Then God told Moses what to do next. God is gracious to give us direction day by day. If an entire year was laid out before us, we might all want to go back to Egypt!

Numbers 13:1-3 And the Lord spoke unto Moses, saying, Send thou men, that they may search the land of Canaan, which I give unto the children of Israel: of every tribe of their fathers shall ye send a man, everyone a ruler among them. And Moses by the commandment of the Lord sent them from the wilderness of Paran:

Knowing what the outcome would be, God left the choice to Moses as to which twelve men to send. Moses knew these hand-picked men well. He then instructed them on exactly where to go and what to do.

Their assignment was to spy and to report on:

- What type land was there
- If the people were weak or strong – few or many
- If the land was good or bad
- If the people lived in cities, camps, or strongholds
- If the land was fat or lean and if it had wood

The remainder of chapter 13 contains the following information: Moses told them to be of good courage and to return with the fruit of the land. He sent them forth during the time of "first-ripe grapes," expecting them to return with a bounty of fresh fruits.

The twelve did as they were instructed and searched the land forty days before returning with their bounty. Twelve men traveling incognito forty days in unfamiliar territory was quite an accomplishment.

Numbers 13:27-28 And they told him (Moses) and said, We came unto the land to which thou sentest us. And surely it floweth with milk and honey; and this fruit is the fruit of it. Nevertheless, the people are strong that dwell in the land, and the cities are walled, and very great: and, moreover, we saw the children of Anak there.

NOTE: **Deuteronomy 9:2** identifies the children of the Anak as being, "A great people and tall ... who can stand before the children of Anak!"

Verse 13:29 lists the other people dwelling in the land God wanted them to conquer: the Amalekites, Hittites, Jebusites, and Canaanites.

That's quite a list! We might easily conclude this was an impossible mission and that requiring these ill-equipped former slaves to do it was totally unreasonable!

Apparently the spies' report was heard by more than just Moses, because in the next verse we're told:

13:30 And Caleb stilled the people before Moses, and said, Let us go up at once, and possess it; for we are well able to overcome it.

Sounds like the people had forgotten God's power demonstrated when He sent ten plagues to their Egyptian captors, parted the mighty Red Sea for their safe escape, and drowned the entire Egyptian army. (We tend to forget how good God has been to us once an "evil report" enters our heart).

13:31-33 But the men who went up with him said, We are not able to go up against the people; for they are stronger than we. And they brought up an evil report of the land, which they had searched, unto the children of Israel, saying, The land, through which we had gone to search it, is a land that eateth up the inhabitants thereof; and all the people that we saw in it are men of great stature, and there we saw the giants, to sons of Anak, who come of the giants; and we were in our own sight as grasshoppers, and so we were in their sights.

Their opinion of themselves may have been accurate, "We were in our own sights as grasshoppers." How would they have seen themselves if looking through the eyes of faith? Yes, the people of Canaan were huge, but they weren't bigger than the God of Israel. In reality, what they said was true. There was no way (apart from God) that they could prevail against these inhabitants. Since their report was true, why did God say it was evil? Because, dear friend, their report revealed that they had no faith in God for which they were without excuse. Those who over-dosed in disbelief spread their contagious fear and unbelief to the entire congregation. What a pitiful sight!

The next verse discloses the effect their report had on the congregation:

14:1 And all congregation lifted up their voice and cried; and the people wept that night.

Here's an indication that we are wallowing in fear, in self-pity, and/or in unbelief – we weep well into the night. We do face much adversity from the cradle to the grave but we have someone who walks with us. And that someone is omnipresent, omnipotent, and has promised to never leave or forsake us. If you have to face the sons of Anak, you won't face them alone, and you won't be defeated.

14:2-4 And all of the children of Israel murmured against Moses and against Aaron: and the whole congregation said unto them, Would God that we had died in the land of Egypt! Or would God we had died in this wilderness! And wherefore hath the Lord brought us unto this land, to fall by the sword, that our wives and our children should be a prey? Were it not better for us to return into Egypt? And they said one to another, Let us make a captain, and let us return into Egypt.

They acknowledged that the Lord had brought them thus far. If they had been able to read a few chapters ahead and learned the judgment for bringing an evil report after surveying for forty days would be forty years of wandering while all the unbelieving died-off, perhaps they would have reconsidered.

14:5-6 Then Moses and Aaron fell on their faces before all the assembly of the congregation of the children of Israel. And Joshua, the son of Nun, and Caleb, the son of Jephunneh, who were of them that searched the land, rent (tore) their clothes;

NOTE: The Biblical custom of renting or tearing clothing when blasphemy was encountered remained prevalent throughout the New Testament too. Barnabus and Paul rent (tore) their clothes when they were hailed as gods. **(Acts 14:11-15)** The magistrates did likewise when they heard that Paul and Silas were accused of blasphemous deeds. **(Acts 16:22)** And the high priest rent (tore) his clothes, and said of Jesus, "He hath spoken blasphemy." **(Matthew 26:65 and Mark 14:63)**

14:7-9 And they (Joshua and Caleb) spoke unto all the company of the children of Israel, saying, The land, in which we passed through to search it, is an exceeding good land. If the Lord delight in us, then he will bring us into this land, and give it us: a land which floweth with milk and honey. Only rebel not against the Lord, neither fear thee the people of the land; for they are bread for us;

their defense is departed from them, and the Lord is with us: fear them not.

These few scriptures identify basic weaknesses among people (of which I am one). Sometimes we are prone to rebel against God, sometimes we are fearful of an enemy or obstacle that we haven't even encountered and are especially vulnerable when we are weary.

The next verse contains our study's second, "But," or objection of the people to the counsel given to them by God's chosen leaders. The first was in **13:31** after God's servant, Caleb, had admonished them to go up and possess the land. Their rejection of his counsel began with "But." The second "But" is when they overruled God's counsel again in **14:10**.

14:10 But all the congregation demanded to stone them with stones.

In the conclusion of this verse, the Lord God Jehovah enters the scene:

14:10 And the glory of the Lord appeared in the tabernacle of the congregation before all the children of Israel.

God had had enough. Notice that His glory appeared in the tabernacle to all of His children. Now they will absolutely be without excuse. At this point, God began a lengthy exchange with His servant Moses. Our study will conclude with verse 38. Let's note that these verses contain five scriptures where God uses the conjunction "But" Himself.

Here is another observance that may be of interest to you. Scripture records at least eight times when God asked, "How long?" Our Creator God who created time for the benefit of mankind and who lives in a timeless realm asked this question far more than any anyone else in scripture. Hmmm.

God then initiated a heart-revealing conversation with Moses that began by His twice asking the question, "How long?"

14:11-12 And the Lord said unto Moses, How long will this people provoke me? And how long will it be before they believe me, for all the signs which I have shown among them? I will smite them with pestilence, and disinherit them, and will make of thee a greater nation and mightier than they.

Disobedience is a serious personal insult with God. Their rejection of Him and His appointed leadership was not acceptable then as it not today.

The following verses contain Mosses' appeal on behalf of his rebellious and discouraged flock:

14:13-19 And Moses said unto the Lord, Then the Egyptians shall hear it (for thou broughtest up this people in thy might from among them), And they will tell it to the inhabitants of this land; for they have heard that thou, Lord, art among this people, that thou, Lord, art seen face to face, and that thy cloud standeth over them, and that thou goest before them, by daytime in a pillar of a cloud, and in a pillar of fire by night. Now if thou shalt kill all this people as one man, then the nations which have heard the fame of thee will speak, saying, Because the Lord was not able to bring this people into the land which he swore to give unto them, therefore he hath slain them in the wilderness. And now, I beseech, let the power of my Lord be great according as though hath spoken, saying, The Lord is long-suffering, and of great mercy, forgiving iniquity and transgression, and by no means clearing the guilty, visiting the iniquity of the fathers upon the children unto the third and fourth generation. Pardon, I beseech thee, the iniquity of this people according unto the greatness of thy mercy, and as thou hast forgiven this people, from Egypt even until now.

Moses noticeably implored no less than five times in the beginning of his plea reminding God of all He had done. Moses then shifted his appeal to God's mercy.
He quoted **Exodus 34:6-7** in asking God to pardon their sins as He had when he returned with the second set of stone engraved commandments.

Moses' uncompromising love for God won him great favor. God then grants full pardon of their sins but with a heavy punishment:
   14:20-23 And the Lord said, I have pardoned according to thy word; But as truly as I live, all the earth shall be filled with the glory of the Lord. Because all those men who have seen my glory, and my miracles which I did in Egypt, and in the wilderness, and have put me to the test

these ten times, and have not harkened to my voice; surely they shall not see the land which I swore to give unto their fathers, neither shall any of them that provoked me see it.

Wow! Having our sins pardoned is such a relief! However, few may realize that every Christian will individually stand before the Judgment seat of Christ when their deeds are judged for recompense. **(Colossians 3:24-25, 1st Corinthians 3:14, 15, 2nd Corinthians 5:9-10)**

We need to pay attention when God says, "Because," before giving His reasoning. (He'll state another "Because" when rewarding Caleb). God said all these men had "provoked" Him. Provoked is a Hebrew word (#5006), meaning "to scorn or despise." He also said that He had "pardoned" them. Pardoned is a Hebrew word (#5545), meaning to "forgive or spare." The Lord further stated that they had disobeyed Him ten times. Their continuous rebellion had topped the Richter scale; now there would retribution with serious and painful consequence. None that had provoked God would see the Promise Land much less enter it.

Numbers 14:24 But my servant, Caleb, because he had another spirit with him, and hath followed me fully, him will I bring into the land where into he went; and his seed shall possess it.

God honored Caleb by calling him "my servant," as He had others such as: Abraham (Isaiah 41:8), Jacob (Isaiah 45:4), and Nebuchadnezzar (Jeremiah 27:6). Without fanfare or trumpets blowing, God stated His reason for rewarding Caleb and his seed: "… because he had another spirit with him, and hath followed me fully." He'll do the same for you, my friend – just be sure you have the right spirit and follow Him fully.

Here's an interesting observation. In the next verse, God directs them straight into enemy territory:

14:25 (Now the Amalekites and the Canaanites dwelt in the valley). Tomorrow turn you, and get you into the wilderness by the way of the Red Sea.

God continued to voice His dissatisfaction to Moses and Aaron:

14:26-27 And the Lord spoke unto Moses and unto Aaron, saying, How long shall I bear with this evil congregation, who murmur against me? I have heard the murmurings of the children of Israel, which they murmur against me.

The sin of unbelief is gross, and is especially gross for those who were chosen to know Him.

14:28-29 Say unto them, As truly as I live, saith the Lord, as you have spoken in my ears, so will I do to you. Your carcasses shall fall in this wilderness; and all who were numbered of you, according to your whole number, from twenty years old and upward, who have murmured against me …

They all lived to see that God meant what He had said.

Hebrews 3:15-19 While it is said, Today if ye will hear his voice, harden not your hearts, as in the provocation. For some (who) when they heard, did provoke? Did not all that came out of Egypt by Moses? But with whom was he grieved forty years? Was it not with them who sinned whose carcasses fell in the wilderness? And to whom swore he that they should not enter into his rest, but to them that believed not? So we see that they could not enter in because of unbelief.

The seriousness of truly believing God, of trusting Him completely, of endeavoring to walk in a way that's pleasing unto Him cannot be over-stressed. Those who do will not be ashamed on Judgment Day.

Numbers 14:30-34 Doubtless ye shall not come into the land, concerning which I swore to make you dwell therein, except Caleb, the son of Jephunneh, and Joshua, the son of Nun. But your little ones, whom ye said should be a prey, them will I bring in, and they shall know the land in which ye have despised. But as for you, your carcasses, they shall fall in this wilderness. And your children shall wander in the wilderness forty years, and bear your whoredoms (harlotries), until your carcasses shall be wasted in this wilderness. After the number of days in which ye searched the land, even forty days, each day for a year, shall ye bear your iniquities, even forty years, and ye shall know my breach of promise.

What severe judgment! The severity of their judgment represents the extent of God's disappointment. I know of times when I have disappointed the God who forgave me and who has delivered me from darkness. In remembering, my heart quakes. But it quakes even more when I remember what the prophet Isaiah wrote of Messiah:

Isaiah 53:6 All we like sheep have gone astray; we have turned every one to his own way; and the Lord hath laid on him the iniquity of us all.

Numbers 14:35 I, the Lord, have said, I will surely do it unto this evil congregation, who are gathered together against me: in this wilderness they shall be consumed, and there they shall die.

God said the entire congregation was evil because they had believed an evil report and had lacked faith in Him. God's people are always to be people of unshakeable faith in the unchanging God. He said their murmuring against His appointed leadership was "against me." Here again was another deep personal insult to God.

14:36-39 And the men, whom Moses sent to search the land, who returned and made all the congregation to murmur against him, by bringing up a slander upon the land. Even those men who did bring up an evil report upon the land, died by the plague before the Lord. But Joshua, the son of Nun, and Caleb, the son of Jephunneh, who were of the men who went in to search the land, lived still. And Moses told these sayings unto all the children of Israel; and the people mourned greatly.

It matters a great deal whose report we believe (have faith in). Those walking closely to God will discern His voice and will not be among those who bring an unbelieving evil report.

This concludes our brief study but certainly does not conclude the long history of God dealing with His own, as He is still doing today.

TRUST OR THRUST?

Even though there are five men named John, which means "Jehovah has been gracious," in the New Testament, only one has been called "the disciple whom Jesus loved." He is described this way five times. **(John 13:23, 19:26, 20:2, 21:7, 21:20)** This John would probably be the one you would call to mind.

He was a fisherman who had been a disciple of John the Baptist before becoming a disciple of the Lord Jesus. He wrote five New Testament books. Church historians and missionaries the world over have said the Gospel of John is the most beloved of all the twenty-nine books of the New Testament. It has been translated into more languages and is thought to have been used to win more converts than any other book.

John's love and devotion to Jesus are especially appreciated. And I especially appreciate his sensitive way of recounting how skillfully Jesus dealt with individuals, such as Thomas.

If you were told that scripture speaks of one Thomas, you might say, "Oh, that was doubting Thomas." We're going to learn that, by the mercy of God, "doubting Thomas" became "believing Thomas."

The apostle Thomas, the subject of our study, is mentioned in scripture twelve times; once in each of the three other gospels, once in the Book of Acts, and eight times in the Gospel of John.

John 20:19-21 Then the same day at evening, being the first day of the week, when the doors were shut where the disciples were assembled for fear of the Jews, came Jesus and stood in the midst, and said unto them, 'Peace be unto you'. And when he had so said, he showed unto them his hands and his side. Then were the disciples glad, when they saw the Lord. Then said Jesus to them again, Peace be unto you; as my Father hath sent me, even so send I you.

(Continuing in verse 24) But Thomas, one of the twelve, called Didymus (twin), was not with them when Jesus came. Didymus is a Greek word (#1324) meaning, "twin, two-fold, or double."

:25-29 The other disciples, therefore, said unto him, We have seen the Lord. But he said unto them, Except I shall see in his hands the print of the nails, and put my finger into the print of the nails, and **thrust** my hand into his side, I will not believe. And after eight days, again his disciples were inside and Thomas with them; then came Jesus, the doors being shut, and stood in the midst, and said, Peace be unto you. Then said he unto Thomas, Reach thy finger, and behold my hands; and reach here thy hand, and **thrust** it into my side; and be not faithless, but believing. And Thomas answered, and said unto him, my Lord and my God. Jesus said unto him, Thomas, because thou hast seen me, thou hast believed; blessed are they that have not seen, and yet have believed. When the others told Thomas that they had seen the Lord, his haughty response reads like a taunt of an unbeliever.

NOTE: The significance of it being the eighth day and the implication of the word "thrust" will be illuminated later.

Jesus repeated the words of Thomas but without condemning him. Absolute awe and adoration surged through Thomas with the comprehension that Jesus was alive, that He was the Son of God, and that he himself was forgiven. These three astonishments are shared by all who come to know Jesus.

Jesus spoke directly to the immediate need of His disciples and said, "Peace be unto you." Scriptures tell of only four times when Jesus spoke these words. And three of those four times are here in these eleven verses. This lets us know how distressed they were and how careful Jesus was to comfort their hearts.

According to **Luke 24:33** there were more disciples present than the eleven; but we're not told how many. Jesus did not upbraid them for being fearful or for not having faith. Instead, He merely supplied what they lacked by saying, "Peace be unto you."

Some have concluded by the words and actions of Thomas before the Lord's resurrection that he was "double-minded and unstable."

James 1:8 A double-minded man is unstable in all his ways.

Prior to Lazarus being raised from the dead:

John 11:16 Then said Thomas, who is called Didymus, unto his fellow disciples. 'Let us also go, that we may die with him.

Thomas wanted to be with Lazarus, who at this point, was dead, when he could have remained with Jesus, who was present in the flesh. Unstable and unbelieving Thomas could not see that to remain by the side of Jesus was greater.

Later after having witnessed that Jesus had raised Lazarus from the dead, he refused to believe that Jesus had risen also. Hmmm.

Remember that Thomas had said:
:25 Except (or unless) I shall see in his hands the print of the nails, and **thrust** my hand into his side, I will not believe.

By saying, "except," he made a stipulation (a condition or requirement) to his believing.

Here are some stipulations or requirements specified by Jesus:
Luke 13:3 I tell you, Nay. But except you repent, ye shall also perish.
John 3:3 ... except a man be born again, he cannot see the kingdom of God.
John 6:44 No man can come to me, except the Father, who hath sent me, draw him.

Matthew 18:3 Verily I say unto you, <u>except</u> ye be converted, and become as little children, ye shall not enter into the Kingdom of heaven.

John 6:53 ... verily, verily, I say unto you, <u>except</u> ye eat the flesh of the Son of man, and drink of his blood, ye have no life in you.

We know that the Word became flesh and dwelt among us. The Bible that you hold in your hands is the word of God. We must eat and be nourished by His flesh daily to be a part of Him.

John 6:65 ... no man can come unto me, <u>except</u> it were given unto him by my Father.

2nd Timothy 2:5 And if any man also strive for masteries, yet he is not crowned, <u>except</u> he strive lawfully.

Thomas said he would not believe <u>except</u> he "see his hands, put my finger in the nail prints, and **thrust** my hand into his side." Thomas would not be satisfied with only a "look-see." His lack of faith - his lack of love for Jesus caused him to want to **thrust** not just a finger, but his entire hand into the Lord's side.

Thrust is a Greek word (#906). The scripture application of this word is <u>always</u> violent and intense. It is the same word used to describe the way Paul and Silas were treated by the Philippian jailer **(Acts 16:24)** when he "<u>**thrust**</u> them into the inner prison." It is disturbing that Thomas would choose such a word to describe the way he wanted to touch Jesus.

Thomas was saying that <u>except</u> he experienced things he could recognize by his senses, he would not believe. He was accustomed to walking by sight, but that would have to change; now he would be required to walk by faith.

What happened in the heart of Thomas during the next eight days? Did the memory of his own words pierce his heart? I believe they did. On the eighth day, Thomas was then found to be with the other disciples - "then came Jesus." **(John 20:26)** Jesus knows just when to arrive. I wondered why eight days; why not three or five? At the beginning of our lesson, I mentioned that the eighth day wait was significant.

The Lord spoke this to Moses as recorded in:
Leviticus 12:3 saying. And in the eighth day the flesh of his foreskin shall be circumcised.

Other scriptures record that Isaac, Jesus, and Paul were all circumcised in the natural on the eighth day of their lives. The circumcision experienced by Thomas on the eighth day was the circumcision of the heart; the circumcision not made with hands.

Deuteronomy 10:16 Circumcise, therefore, the foreskin of your heart, and be no more stiff-necked.

Stiff-necked is a Greek word (#4644) meaning "obstinate, unreasonably determined to have one's own way, not yielding to reason."

These words were spoken by Stephen moments before his martyrdom:

Acts 7:51 Ye stiff-necked and uncircumcised in heart and ears, ye do always resist the Holy Ghost; as your fathers did, so do ye.

We all need the continual inward circumcision of the heart spoken of by Paul. This is what Thomas lacked until the eighth day.

Romans 8:28-29 For he is not a Jew who is one outwardly; neither is that circumcision which is outward in the flesh; but he is a Jew who is one inwardly; and circumcision is that of the heart, in the spirit and not in the letter; whose praise is not of men, but of God.

Thomas' answer revealed his heart was overwhelmed. Only once does scripture record someone making the statement he made on the eighth day: "My Lord and my God." **(John 20:28)** He had received the circumcision not made with hands spoken of by Paul in **Colossians 2:11**.

The last mention of Thomas is in **Acts 1:13** where we learn that he abode in the upper room with the other apostles. Yes, Thomas had learned to abide; to hang in there, not to wander off in doubt and fear, and not to be separated from the fold. He had received corrective reproof of the Lord.

As you walk with the Lord, welcome His corrective reproof as a means of His perfecting you.

Proverbs 15:31 The ear that heareth the reproof of life <u>abideth</u> among the wise.

Here's a tasty nugget from the Lord.

In the following verse the word <u>accept</u> is used twice and the word <u>abide</u> is used three times.

John 15:4 <u>Abide</u> in me, and I in you. As the branch cannot bear fruit of itself, <u>except</u> it <u>abide</u> in the vine, no more can ye <u>except</u> ye <u>abide</u> in me.

This message is presented in a palatable way to help you understand that what you consider to be your "exceptions" (i.e. Except God do this, except this happens this way, and on and on) will not matter at all when you truly <u>abide</u> in Him.

Those who trust have no desire to thrust.

WATCH and PRAY

2nd Timothy 3:16 All scripture is given by inspiration of God, and is profitable for doctrine, for reproof, for correction, for instruction in righteousness.

The Bible is God's inspired word and His word is truth. Yet we know it is not hard for mockers to find fault.

Scriptures, like the following, can seem contradictory:
Matthew 2:23 ... He shall be called a Nazarene
Matthew 2:15 ... Out of Egypt I have called my son
Luke 2:11 For unto you is born this day in the city of David a Savior, who is Christ the Lord
Luke 1:31 (Gabriel) ... and shalt call his name JESUS
Isaiah 7:14 ... and shall call his name Immanuel
Psalm 121:3 ... he who keepeth thee will not slumber
Mark 4:38 And he was in the stern of the boat, asleep on a pillow; and they awake him, and say unto him, Master, carest thou not that we perish?

Obviously, God performed His word in His way and in His time. Our study, "Watch and Pray," will seem to contradict the following scriptures:

Acts 20:35 ... It is more blessed to give than to receive
Matthew 10:8 ... freely ye have received, freely give
Matthew 5:42 Give unto him that asketh thee, and from him that would borrow of thee turn not away.
Proverbs 21:26 ...but righteous giveth and spareth not.

2nd Corinthians 9:7 Every man according as he has purposed in his heart, so let him give, not grudgingly, or of necessity; for God loveth a cheerful giver.

Luke 6:38 Give and it shall be given unto you; good measure, pressed down, and shaken together, and running over, shall men give into your bosom. For with what measure that ye measure it shall be measured to you again.

These scriptures are all God's word, and they are all truth; however, we are going to examine a well-known parable that tells the church that it <u>must possess</u>.

The Parable of the Ten Virgins

God gave clear understanding of His requirements for His Son's Bride in the parable of the ten virgins. The parable begins with ten friends of the bride waiting in the bride's house (the church) for the expected arrival of the bridegroom.

Matthew 25:1-4 Then shall the kingdom of heaven be likened unto ten virgins, who took their lamps and went forth to meet the bridegroom. And five of them were wise and five were foolish. They that were foolish took their lamps and took no oil with them; but the wise took oil in their vessels with their lamps.

By the following verse, we understand that all ten virgins had the word of God.
Psalm 119:105 Thy word is a lamp unto my feet, and a light unto my path.

Oil in scripture often represents the anointing of God: **Exodus 30:25** speaks of a holy anointing oil. In **Exodus 27:20** the children of Israel were commanded to bring pure olive oil so that the tabernacle lamp would burn continuously.

In **Matthew 12:4** Note that the five wise virgins brought oil in their vessels with their lamps. In scripture, our bodies are sometimes called vessels.

1st Thessalonians 4:4 ... everyone of you should know how to possess his vessel in sanctification and honor.

The Lord speaking of Paul in **Acts 9:15** ... he is a chosen vessel unto me.

2nd Corinthians 4:7 But we have this treasure (knowledge of God) in earthen vessels that the excellency of the power may be of God, and not of us.

Matthew 25:5 While the bridegroom tarried, they all slumbered and slept.

Here's a thought: had the bridegroom arrived at the expected time, all the virgins would have been ready. While He tarried, those who were absolutely chaste and devoted remained ready; those who were complacent were caught unprepared.

What about the phrase, "they all slumbered"? Surely the Lord's Bride is not characterized by slumber (sleeping on the job) or in some sort of lethargic stupor. When speaking this parable, Jesus may have been revealing that his Bride was prepared and that she was resting in Him.

25:6-7 And at midnight there was a cry made: Behold, the bridegroom cometh; go ye out to meet him. Then all those virgins arose and trimmed their lamps.

They all were awaken by the call, and they all went forth. If you want your lamp to burn brighter, the wick must be trimmed. And that's exactly what they did! Christians, be sure to keep your lamps trimmed and burning!

25:8-9 And the foolish said unto the wise, give us your oil, for our lamps have gone out. But the wise answered, saying, Not so, lest there be not enough for us and you; but go ye rather to them that sell, and buy for yourselves.

Six scriptures listed at the beginning of our lessen instructed us to always give. But here we find that the five wise virgins were not able to give their precious oil to the five foolish virgins. Instead, they told them to, "go ... and buy for yourselves." That may not seem harsh or callous when we examine the following scriptures:

Proverbs 9:12 If thou be wise, thou shalt be wise for thyself; but if thou scoffest, thou alone shalt bear it.

Notice in the following verse that the words oil, wise, and foolish are found.

Proverbs 21:20 There is treasure to be desired, and <u>oil</u>, in the dwelling of the <u>wise</u> but a <u>foolish</u> man spendeth it up.

This verse reveals more of God's wisdom:
Proverbs 23:23 Buy the truth, and sell it not; also wisdom, and instruction, and understanding.

We purchase God's truth, wisdom, and understanding by laying down our lives before Him as a daily sacrifice. All we have to offer Him are our lives which aren't even our own since we were bought with a price: His precious redeeming Blood.

The foolish virgins had no more days to give in exchange for their souls. They had not been willing to lay down their lives daily in exchange (or in trade) for wisdom and understanding; thus they were not ready (or prepared) to enter His Kingdom.

Proverbs 3:13-14 Happy is the man that findeth wisdom, and the man that getteth understanding; for the merchandise of it is better than the merchandise of silver, and the gain thereof than fine gold.

The Hebrew word (#5504) "merchandise" means, "trade."

Matthew 16:26 and Mark 8:37 ... what shall a man give in exchange for his soul?
Matthew 25:10 And while they went to buy, the bridegroom came, and <u>they that were ready</u> went in with him to the marriage, and the door was shut.

We are not told who shut the door. In a sense, the unprepared virgins caused the door to be shut by their steadfast refusal to not love God as they should. It's an open and shut case; a door once opened had been shut.

1st John 2:28 And, now little children, <u>abide in him</u>, that, when he shall appear, we may have confidence and not be <u>ashamed before him at his coming</u>.

This study is meant to encourage the Bride who has made herself ready and also to challenge those who have not.

Revelation 19:7-8 Let us be glad and rejoice, and give honor to him; for the marriage of the Lamb is come, and <u>his wife has made herself ready</u>. And to her was granted that she should be arrayed in fine linen, clean, and white; for the fine linen is the righteousness of the saints.

ALL parables foretelling of His second coming include the element of surprise making preparedness a prerequisite of utmost importance:
 Luke 12:40 Be ye, therefore, ready also; for the Son of man cometh at an hour when ye think not.
 Mark 13:33 Take heed, watch and pray; for ye know not when the time is.
 Matthew 24:36 But of that day and hour knoweth no man ...
 Matthew 24:42,44 Watch, therefore; for ye know not what hour our Lord doth come. Therefore be ye also ready; for in such an hour as ye think not the Son of man cometh.

These warnings are not given in parables directed to tribulation saints who will have ample signs preceding Christ's return, when His coming will be marked by many visible signs. When He comes for His Bride, <u>who has made herself ready</u>, a large portion of the visible church will be unprepared, and will be ashamed at His coming.

Jesus spoke these words to the religious Jews and recorded in:
John 5:39, 40, 42 Search the scriptures; for in them ye think ye have eternal life; and they are they which testify of me. And ye will not come unto me, that ye might have life. But I know you, that you have not the love of God in you.

These Jews had the word of God; they didn't have the love of God. Who and what you love is all that matters, my friend. Yes, some may have a love for God, but do not love Him more than the things of this world.

Here are the concluding verses in the Parable of the Ten Virgins:
Matthew 25:11-13 Afterward came also the other virgins, saying, Lord, Lord, open to us! But he answered and said, Verily, I say unto you, <u>I know you not</u>. Watch therefore, for ye know neither the day nor the hour wherein the Son of man cometh.

The Bible quotes Jesus three separate times saying, "I know you not," or "I never knew you." **(Matthew 7:23, 25:12, Luke 13:27)** On each occasion, He was rejecting people who were attempting to enter His Kingdom and who were found to be unworthy.

The five wise virgins journeyed forth ready to meet Him not only because they had the word of God, but also because they had holy anointing oil within their vessels (themselves). A word to the wise: this required oil is acquired as we daily dwell in His presence.

WE DON'T DRINK COFFEE IN THIS CHURCH

Weary from an over-booked schedule (thanks to his wife), Brother Travis drove down one wrong country road after another searching for the rural church. The sun seemed to be setting faster than usual as his anxiety level increased even faster. "These folk will understand. I'm not the only minister/musician to have gotten lost looking for their off-the-map church," he mused.

There it was sitting beside the road with a parking lot already mostly full. His delayed arrival left little time to set up musical equipment and check the church's sound system. Brother Travis thought, "That's okay. At least I made it." Great, some church members surmised the situation and pitched in to help unload while he made his way to their fellowship hall envisioning only of how wonderful a cup of hot coffee would be. Brother Travis felt for sure he had gotten a whiff of freshly brewed coffee. What a sensory serenade that was to the weary traveler. (Or so he thought).

Rounding a corner of the fellowship hall doorway, his eyes surveyed the room. What, no coffee? Seeing a woman in the room, he asked where the coffee was. Her prideful snap caught him off guard, "We don't drink coffee in this church!" Stunned and still longing for coffee, he turned to leave and found himself face-to-face with a bigger-than-life Coke machine.

When I heard Brother Travis relate this story, I prayed, "Lord, deliver me from religion." It can be scary when we hear about believers making a mountain out of a mole hill.

Paul's speech before Areopagus, the highest court in Athens, is a priceless challenge to those led by their intellect or carnal understanding. He began by saying:

Acts 17:22 Then Paul stood in the midst of Mars' Hill, and said, Ye men of Athens, I perceive that in all things ye are too superstitious (or too religious).

Here we are today more than two thousand years later and some are still majoring on (focusing on) what may not matter. Being "too superstitious" is the not the way to win souls.

Proverbs 14:25 A true witness delivereth souls ...

Matthew 7:1-2 Judge not, that ye be not judged. For with what judgment ye judge, ye shall be judged; and with what measure ye measure, it shall be measured to you again.

Christians should be stepping stones and not stumbling blocks.

Well, say, "Ouch" or "Amen."

WE'LL TAKE HIM IN A HEARTBEAT

One of the operating surgeons said to the other, "We're losing him." Then one of the two angels standing by and ministering to Bill Johnston said, "We'll take him in a heartbeat." But in a split-second decision, the physicians renewed their efforts and were able to successfully complete Bill's heart surgery.

Suffering heart failure, nearly dying on an operating table, hearing doctors comment on how he wasn't going to make it, and seeing and hearing angels speak wasn't what Bill had given any prior thought to. Later, as he recovered in the hospital, he had a vivid memory of all that had occurred.

Though he had loved and served the Lord throughout his life, he had been plagued by the fear of death. Perhaps this fear had been a result of losing his father at an early age. But, whatever the root cause, the Lord mercifully put a stop to its torment the moment the angel spoke. Bill Johnston lived the remainder of his days in peace.

Imagine how brief a time a heartbeat is. An adult heart beats between sixty and a hundred times per minute. The angel had said, "We'll take him in a heartbeat."

These scriptures speak of Jesus who took on the robe of flesh that he might destroy death:
Hebrews 2:14-15 Forasmuch, then, as the children are partakers of flesh and blood, he also himself likewise took part of the same, that through death he might destroy

him that had (past tense) the power of death, that is, the devil, and deliver them who, through fear of death, were all their lifetime subject to bondage.

Job 14:14-15 ... All the days of my appointed time will I wait, till my change come. Thou shalt call, and I will answer thee; thou wilt have a desire to the work of thine own hands.

Bill Johnston's change came twelve years later on August 6, 2008, when God had a desire to the work of His own hands. Believing God's word, Bill slipped from this life into the everlasting arms of Jesus, as angels did as they had spoken; they took him in a heartbeat.

WHY A FOX?

Luke 13:31 states that as Jesus journeyed toward Jerusalem, certain Pharisees warned him to flee Herod's jurisdiction cautioning: "Get thee out, and depart from here; for Herod will kill thee."

Let's not fast-forward through that verse without noting that it was Pharisees who warned Jesus. Jesus was in no way intimidated even though He knew the Jewish-by-name-only King Herod had already had John the Baptist killed. Herod (Antipas) remained in relentless antagonism toward Jesus following John's martyrdom.

This may have been fueled by his guilt in having executed a man whom Jesus had said:
Luke 8:28 ... Among those that are born of women there is not a greater prophet than John the Baptist.

In classic cannonball candor, Jesus responded to the Pharisees' warning:
Luke 13:32 Go, and tell that fox, Behold, I cast out devils, and I do cures today and tomorrow, and the third day <u>I shall have finished</u>.

His response contained intriguing statements. One noun is of special interest and caused me to wonder. Why did He say that Herod was a fox? Why not a snake? Why not a dog? He could have referred to him as a scorpion since scorpions are easily made angry, often cause death, and actually destroy each other. But He chose to identify Herod as a fox.

Here's a list of fox behaviors:
> They are mainly nocturnal. (Active at night)
> They stalk their prey with stealth and patience.
> They have very keen sight, hearing, and smell.
> They are fast and catch their prey by outrunning it.
> They often play with their catch before killing it.
> They crouch at the feet of a dominant animal.

For a sacrificial lamb to be accepted by God as a sin offering, it had to be publicly observed for three days, examined, and designated to be without spot or blemish. **(Exodus 12, Leviticus 1, Deuteronomy 15:21)**

Jesus was publicly observed in Jerusalem for three days before being offered as the spotless sacrificial Lamb of God. **(John 12:12)**

Luke 9:31 Moses and Elijah, who appeared in glory, and spoke of his decease <u>which he should accomplish</u> at Jerusalem.

Jesus told the Pharisees in **John 10:17-18** that no man would take His life but that He would lay it down for His lambs in obedience to God.

The last of seven statements He made while impaled to the cross was:
John 19:30 When Jesus, therefore, had received the vinegar, he said, <u>It is finished</u>; and bowed his head, and gave up the spirit.

This was the message He had sent to Herod: "and the third day, <u>I shall have finished</u>." **(Luke 13:32)**

Hebrews 10:12 But this man, after he had offered one sacrifice for sins forever, sat down on the right hand of God ...

Herod was outfoxed by a Lamb; the spotless Lamb of God whose blood was shed once and for all. The redemption of man was complete upon His sacrificial death.

1st Peter 1:19-21 (We were redeemed) ... with the precious blood of Christ, as of a lamb without blemish and without spot, who verily was foreordained before the foundation of the world, but was manifest in these last times for you, <u>who by him do believe in God</u>, who raised him up from the dead and gave him glory, <u>that your faith and hope may be in God</u>.

By His atoning blood sacrifice, we are reconciled to God, made acceptable to Him, welcomed into His eternal kingdom, and <u>by Him do believe in God</u>.

The outfoxed Herod's long-held desire to meet Jesus and to question Him was granted. Following His arrest, Pilate having found no fault in Jesus, and learning He was from Herod's jurisdiction, sent Him unto him.

Luke 23:8 And when Herod saw Jesus, he was exceedingly glad; for he was desirous to see him for a long time, because he had heard many things of him; and he hoped to see some miracle done by him. Then he questioned him in many words; but he answered him nothing.

Jesus didn't answer the king whom He had said was a fox. Undoubtedly, that outfoxed king has answered to the king of Kings; the perfect Lamb of God. Just as a fox is known to crouch at the feet of his dominant foe, so has the outfoxed king.

Philippians 2:9-10 Wherefore, God also hath highly exalted him, and given him the name that is above every name, which is above every name, that at the name of Jesus every knee should bow ...

Song of Solomon 2:15 Take us the foxes, the little foxes that spoil the vines; for our vines have tender grapes.

"Take" is a Hebrew word (#270) meaning, "to catch and hold." If we ignorantly or arrogantly allow the little foxes to spoil our vines, the tender fruits of our life and labor are spoiled. Little foxes can be bitterness, resentment, anger, vanity, or any number of things which seep into and then out of our hearts.

John 15:16 Ye have not chosen me. But I have chosen, you and ordained you, that ye should go and bring forth fruit, and <u>that your fruit should remain</u> ...

WORDS PAINT A PICTURE

The Bible frequently uses "picture words" to describe what otherwise might be difficult to comprehend. For example; the word "like", is a comparative used to paint a picture of what is commonly known of what isn't commonly known.

Since we all have experienced the feeling of a rushing wind, Luke used "like" as a comparative to describe the moving of the Holy Ghost. He wrote:
Acts 2:2 And suddenly there came a sound from heaven <u>like a mighty rushing wind</u> and it filled all the house where they were sitting.

The book of Psalms uses the term, "like" thirty-two times to build images to aid the reader's comprehension. We know what it is to pour water, and we know that when wax is melted it loses its form. King David used the word "like" twice in the following Messianic psalm to describe the suffering of Jesus at Calvary:
Psalm 22:14 I am <u>poured out like water</u>, and all my bones are out of joint; my heart is <u>like wax</u>; it is melted within me.

Likewise, we know that a vessel, created to hold and transport liquid, is virtually useless and has no value once it's broken. King David draws this comparison when describing himself to the Lord:
Psalm 31:12 I am forgotten as a dead man out of mind; I am <u>like</u> a broken vessel.

King David also wrote the following:
Psalm 37:35 I have seen the wicked in great power, and spreading himself <u>like a green bay tree</u>.

Bay trees thrive in hot climates that provide a slow steady growth rate. The bay tree can spread outward while reaching a height of up to 60' producing a massive appearance. King David compared the calculated strategy of a wicked person to the spreading outward and upward of the bay tree.

In Psalm 17, King David used the imagery of a greedy lion, waiting to pounce upon its prey, knowing that his enemies did the same:
    Psalm 17:12 Like a lion greedy of his prey, and as it were a young lion lurking in secret places.

The well-known first Psalm causes the reader to envision a tree planted by rivers of water as a picturesque illustration of a godly man:
    Psalm 1:3 And he shall be like a tree planted by the rivers of water, that bringeth forth its fruit in its season; its leaf also shall not wither; and whatsoever he doeth shall prosper.

Because we have seen well-nourished fruit trees, we can appreciate that a godly man flourishes in the same way:
    Psalm 92:12 The righteous shall flourish like the palm tree; he shall grow like a cedar in Lebanon.

Trees known as "the cedars of Lebanon," the national iconic symbol of Lebanon, are majestic in appearance. Both Bible temples were built using wood from these evergreen giants. Known for their resilience, they live thousands of years with their massive trunks measuring a diameter of six feet. Palm trees have been known to flourish in the Middle East for 5,000 years. Being deeply rooted and, yet, flexible, equips them to endure droughts as well as strong winds.

What a blessing for God's word to declare that the righteous (one who has the imputed righteousness of Jesus) shall flourish like a palm tree and shall grow like a cedar of Lebanon.

The Epistle of James

In his brief epistle, James used the word "like" four times to draw comparisons; twice in the opening chapter.

James 1:6 (speaking of someone who lacks wisdom) But let him ask in faith, nothing wavering. For he that wavereth is <u>like</u> a wave of the sea driven with the wind and tossed.

James 1:23-24 For if any man be a hearer of the word, and not a doer, he is <u>like</u> a man beholding his natural face in a mirror. For he beholdeth himself, and goeth his way, and immediately forgetteth what manner of man he was.

Here's an interesting contrast:

In the following scriptures, he chose <u>not</u> to use the word "like" as he identified what a tongue is and what it can do:

James 3:5-6,8 Even so the tongue is a little member and boasteth great things. Behold, how great a matter a little fire kindleth! And the tongue <u>is</u> a fire, a world of iniquity; so <u>is</u> the tongue among our members that it defileth the whole body, and setteth on fire the course of nature, and it is set on fire of hell. But the tongue can no man tame; it <u>is</u> an unruly evil, full of deadly poison

Once spoken, words cannot be unspoken.

WRAPPED IN WHITE LINEN

Each of the four gospels tells of the Body of Jesus being wrapped in linen by Joseph of Arimathaea. The gospel of John includes Nicodemus who assisted Joseph.

Matthew 27:59 And when Joseph had taken the Body, he wrapped it in a clean linen cloth ...

Mark 15:43,46 Joseph, of Arimathaea, an honorable counselor, who also waited for the Kingdom of God, came, and went in boldly unto Pilate, and asked for the Body of Jesus. And he (Joseph of Arimathaea) <u>bought</u> fine linen, and took him down, and wrapped him in the linen ...

Luke 23:50-53 And, behold, there was a man named Joseph, a counselor; and he was a good and righteous man. (The same had not consented to the counsel and deed of them); he was of Arimathaea, a city of the Jews, who also waited for the Kingdom of God. This man went unto Pilate and begged the Body of Jesus. And he took it down, and wrapped it in linen ...

John 19:40 Then took they (Joseph and Nicodemus) the Body of Jesus, and wound it in linen clothes ...

The following information emphasizes the importance of Jesus being wrapped in linen:
    Sacred vestments of priests were made of linen.
    Pharaoh arrayed Joseph in linen to honor him.
    Scriptures refer to linen as the "yarn of Egypt."
    Revelation 15:6 reveals that angels are clothed

in white linen as a symbol of moral purity.

Luke 16:19 refers to fine linen as a sign of luxury.

THE BRIDE IS TO BE HONORED

Revelation 19:6-8 And I heard, as it were, the voice of a great multitude, and like the voice of many waters, and like the voice of mighty peals of thunder, saying, Hallelujah! For the Lord God omnipotent reigneth. Let us be glad and rejoice, and give honor unto him; for the marriage of the Lamb is come, and his wife has made herself ready. And to her was granted that she should be arrayed in fine linen, clean and white; for fine linen is the righteousness of saints.

No Jewish person is embalmed following death; instead, a three-person team performs a "Taharah." The Taharah is a sacred rite of washing and purifying of the body while reciting prayers and psalms before performing a "Tachrichim" by dressing the deceased in a <u>pure white 100% linen</u> burial garment also called a shroud which is a hooded robe. This white linen burial garment is used for every deceased Jewish person regardless of the person's status or age in life. This custom was begun in 70 CE (meaning Common Era and is the same year as 70 A.D.) This burial garment is hand-stitched without adding buttons, zippers, or clasps.

Caskets are made to disengage quickly. Holes are drilled in the casket's bottom to accelerate decomposition. This is done in harmony with:

Genesis 3:19 ... thou (shall) return unto the ground; for out of it wast thou taken: for dust thou art, and unto dust thou shalt return.

Many Christian churches hold what's known as a Baby Dedication Ceremony. The parents bring their infant or young child to the church altar accompanied by near-relatives. The pastor then lays hands on the infant and prays a blessing upon its family and dedicates the infant to the Lord's service. This is an important event for the infant and its family. Just as Joseph and Mary presented the Christ-child to the Lord in the temple at Jerusalem. **(Luke 1:21-39)**

As an added blessing for the infant and its family, I enjoy giving a white linen dedication blanket embroidered (by a friend) with the infant's name and date of birth. Come what may in this child's life, the parents, family, and child will know that it was committed to the Lord wrapped in linen pure and white.

2nd Timothy 1:12 ... for I know whom I have believed and am persuaded that he is able to keep that which I have committed unto him ...

YOU CAN'T HAVE IT!

It was strange; really strange. And quite unexpected too. You know from experience how you feel when the Lord disrupts your current reality to super interject something He wants you to understand.

Before the Sunday evening service began, I had knelt praying at a front row pew while facing the back of the church. The vision God shared is as clear in my mind now as it was years ago. He said, "There are those standing here who will hear me say depart." It was shocking. I jerked my head downward wanting this scene to go away. Without opening my eyes, I saw the customary men standing by the sound booth at the back of the sanctuary. And I understood these were the men He spoke of. When I arose to my feet, I briefly glanced and saw exactly what He had shown. They resembled a hedgerow. They were church members whose attendance was faithful – two were board members. The thought that none knew his true destiny made me hang my head in a crushing silence. The alarming memory lingers to this day.

There were a number of people in that church who were troubled and who caused trouble which made it more of an arena than an actual church. Demons jockeyed for control causing turmoil and schisms. It surely wasn't an environment conducive to healthy Christian growth.

James 3:16 For where envying and strife are, there is confusion and every evil work.

One evening as a prayer meeting was concluding, the Lord again allowed me to see a horrific scene. He shared a view of what was happening in His throne room. Our nemesis old slough-foot himself was berating God marching back and forth while shaking his fist and shouting, "You can't have it! You can't have a people who will walk before you in peace, unity, and love!" He then jumped up and down like an imp on a pogo stick still screaming madly. I bounded to God's defense, and, in my spirit, screamed, "Oh yes, He can! And He can start with me. I will walk with His people in peace, unity and love!" I have sincerely endeavored to do so.

Before long my husband and I were catapulted out of there by the mercies of God. The pastor was then found to be in adultery and resigned. Wounded lambs were scattered. God's heart was broken again.

Those who are faithful to God and who serve Him without compromise won't be ashamed on Judgment Day.